Not a Tame Lion

Not a Tame Lion

A Lent course based on the writings
of C. S. Lewis

HILARY BRAND

DARTON · LONGMAN + TODD

First published in 2008 by
Darton, Longman and Todd Ltd
1 Spencer Court
140–142 Wandsworth High Street
London SW18 4JJ

Reprinted 2012

ISBN-10: 0–232–52700–8
ISBN-13: 978–0–232–52700–1

A catalogue record for this book is available
from the British Library.

Designed and produced by Sandie Boccacci
Set in 9.5/11.5pt Times New Roman
Printed and bound in Great Britain by
Bell & Bain ltd., Glasgow

Contents

Week Four: Living with what we've been given

Week Five: Living with absence

Holy Week

Optional Extra: Living in a sceptical age (Prince Caspian)

Leaders' Notes

Introduction

Preparing for an uncomfortable Lent

We would all like a religion that kept us within our comfort zone. But just as the Aslan of the Narnia stories is not a tame lion,[1] neither is the Christ of the gospels always a comfortable Saviour, saying and doing things that are often unexpected and challenging.

Nor is this a comfortable Lent course. In following the writings of C. S. Lewis, and using films based on them, it leads inexorably to some difficult subjects – suffering, God's absence and hell – as well as some that are distinctly unfashionable – heaven, sin, judgement and the Devil.

Lent, of course, was never intended to be a time of comfort. It was traditionally a time of sackcloth and ashes, of rumblings in the stomach and quiverings of the strained will. It was meant to be a drab grey run-up to the glorious resurrection theme of Easter and the seasonal outburst of sunshine, spring flowers and lambs.

Discomfort is much less fashionable nowadays, especially as an aid to spiritual health and beauty (although, curiously, any amount of discomfort seems to be allowable in the pursuit of toned muscles, size 6 jeans or a wrinkle-free smile).

But I hope that whatever your Lenten attitude to chocolate, sex, alcohol or even Turkish Delight, you will, for this Lent at least, be willing to submit your spirit to a little bit of mental exercise and your mind to a little bit of spiritual challenge. For while C. S. Lewis acknowledges that Christianity is 'a thing of unspeakable comfort', he suggests that this is not where it begins. Rather it often starts with 'dismay'. If you begin by searching for truth, you may well find comfort as a by-product. But if you search for comfort you are in danger of missing both comfort and truth.[2]

Why this book?

There have been times when I wondered whether this book was a good idea. There are a lot of C. S. Lewis experts out there, and I make no claim to be one of them. So I'm pretty sure that it will not fulfil the expectations of Lewis purists.

But I also suspect there are others, unfamiliar with Lewis except as a weaver of children's fantasy tales, who may find his other writings a little academic, dated, male-dominated and occasionally irritating. It may not be quite the gentle inspirational approach they would want their Lent course to take.

So not only am I setting myself up as a commentator on one of the greatest Christian writers of the twentieth century, but I'm running the risk of alienating at least half my potential audience before I start. I decided it was a risk worth taking.

What set me on this trail was when a friend shared the story of her spiritual journey. It was reading the books of C. S. Lewis, she said, that helped her to make sense of Christianity and lead her into faith. That had been some twenty or thirty years ago, and it reminded me of how helpful the books had been to me around that time, and how they had lain unread on the shelf since.

So I started to re-read. And despite struggling through a few rocky seams of convoluted argument, I realised I was discovering nuggets of gold. And I wondered how I could encourage others to go digging.

What this book is not

This is not an anthology of the writings of C. S. Lewis. Nor is it a summary of his writings or a critique of his worldview.

Neither is the Lewis tag simply an excuse to discuss issues thrown up by some good films.

I suppose it is somewhere in between – using the films as a great starting point for delving into some of the issues that Lewis himself thought important, seeing what he had to say on them and wondering what his thoughts have to say to us, half a century after he wrote them.

The films, of course, are not entirely faithful to their original source and so, where necessary, I have tried to clarify what Lewis actually said, wrote and did, as distinct from the silver-screen version. The differences throw some interesting light not just on Hollywood, but on the contemporary culture it seeks to please. And they may well throw into sharp relief Lewis's willingness to be contentious rather than comforting where necessary. He was certainly more than a pedlar of easy answers to difficult questions. He lays this clearly on the line in his great introduction to faith, *Mere Christianity*:

> All I am doing is to ask people to face the facts – to understand the questions which Christianity claims to answer. And they are very terrifying facts. I wish it was possible to say something more agreeable. But I must say what I think is true …[3]

The great thing about Lewis, though, is that he approaches these difficult issues with such wit, logic and vivid imagery that he carries us along with him. Where a lesser writer might just alienate, Lewis provokes us to think outside our comfort zone and so to expand our understanding of God.

What is true of Lewis as an advocate for Christianity is even more true of the Man who began it. When Jesus spoke he used humour, metaphor and astringency in abundance. Like Aslan, he neither was nor is predictable or safe. But also like Aslan, when he comes on the scene, lives that seemed frozen by fear, fault or failure melt beneath his gaze.

So this course looks not just at Lewis's writings on Christianity, but what its founder actually said. Each session links the themes back into the words of the gospels, and each chapter explores not just the writings of C. S. Lewis but the relevant sayings of Jesus and the thoughts of those who were his forerunners and followers, as gathered in the Old and New Testaments.

This course, then, may not always be comfortable. But I hope it will always be stimulating. If it leads you on to explore some of Lewis's books for yourself, then it will have done its job. And if it leads you on to learn more of him who Lewis counted as Lord, then that will be even better.

How the course works

This book offers five weekly group sessions, each with two accompanying chapters to be read individually, before and after the session. Each group session is timed to be about an hour and a half long (but could easily stretch to two hours). Each includes two film clips: one from *Shadowlands* and one from *The Chronicles of Narnia: The Lion, the Witch and the Wardrobe*. It is possible to follow the course without having seen the movies beforehand, but ideally participants should make a point of seeing both movies right through before the course starts.

At the end is a meditative service which brings together the words of Lewis and the story of Easter in an exploration of its central theme of death and rebirth.

There is also an additional, optional weekly session (placed after the meditative service) based around the film *The Chronicles of Narnia: Prince Caspian*. This can be slotted in before Easter or perhaps preferably used as a follow-up session afterwards.

This course covers painful subjects, where participants may have raw feelings. It also covers difficult subjects, where there may be a range of strong opinions. It is essential then, right at the beginning, to approach group sessions with respect and sensitivity towards others. This is not to say that such subjects should be tiptoed around. The whole point of this course is that it allows people to be totally honest and to talk about issues often avoided. This means that others in the group need to be accepted for who they are and where they are, that differences need to be embraced and diversity valued as the great teacher it can so often be.

Suggested ground rules for group sessions

- Give space for every member of the group who wishes to speak to do so.
- Speak as much as possible from your experience, rather than at a theoretical level.
- Actively listen to each contribution, rather than thinking about what you would like to say.
- Respect each other's viewpoints and, if possible, try to understand what formed them.
- Make it a rule that nothing that is said within the group is repeated outside. Make it a safe place to be honest.

Background

Discovering the man and his world

A world at war

When I first saw the movie of *The Lion, the Witch and the Wardrobe*, I was surprised that what only takes a sentence in the book – the children going to the house in the country because of the London air raids – became such a long opening sequence.

But as I've thought about it, I've realised that the wartime world so instantly understood by Lewis's first readers is quite foreign to us now. Over sixty years later his words still have much to say to us, but we will understand them better if we grasp a little of the world from which he and they came.

The Lion, the Witch and the Wardrobe was published in 1950, just five years after the end of the Second World War, although the idea probably first came when Lewis himself was hosting some of those evacuee children. It was right in the midst of wartime that Lewis wrote his most famous non-fiction works: *Mere Christianity* (first given as radio talks), *The Screwtape Letters* and *The Problem of Pain*, during a time when bombs were falling, men were enlisting to fight and many ordinary people were struggling to make sense of pain, suffering and loss.

At this time a very real and powerful evil threatened to engulf the world. It was a time of many journeys into unknown territories, and of food shortages and blackouts, when winter after winter went by with little in the way of Christmas to brighten them. It was also a time when a strong code of decency, duty and good neighbourliness prevailed.

A world of men

The beginning of the film *Shadowlands* shows another aspect of Lewis's world. As the dons, together with row on row of rugby-playing undergraduates, gather to dine in their Oxford college, we realise that this is an almost entirely *male* world. And his writing certainly reflects this, sometimes uncomfortably chauvinistically to my post-feminist ears. Indeed, he speaks of his dislike of both women who prattle foolishly[1] and those who dominate, assuming that 'most of us' feel the same.[2] He maintained that wives should obey their husbands, although aware even then that opinions on this were beginning to change.[3]

Perhaps we will understand him better, though, if we realise that his mother died when he was only nine years old. He lived thereafter with only his father and brother, or in a series of all-male boarding schools. And to rehabilitate him a little, it is worth noting that when he eventually found deep love and marriage late in life, he described his wife Joy Gresham lyrically as:

> … my pupil and my teacher, my subject and my sovereign, and always holding these in solution, my trusty comrade, friend, shipmate, fellow soldier.[4]

A world of books

Clive Staples Lewis, otherwise known as Jack, grew up in middle-class Belfast in the Edwardian era, a lost age of innocence before the disillusionment of the First World War. Occasionally his examples remind us of this lost age, as when he writes of a mother telling her children to tidy the 'schoolroom' and then going to find 'the Teddy Bear and the ink and the French Grammar all lying in the grate'.[5]

He describes himself as:

> … the product of long corridors, empty sunlit rooms, upstairs indoor silences, attics explored in solitude, distant noises of gurgling cisterns and pipes and the noise of wind under the tiles.[6]

His was also a home filled with books and he was certainly an avid reader, devouring *Paradise Lost* at the age of nine. By the age of 17 he was described by his tutor as having read more classics that anyone he had ever known.[7]

His formal education, however, was far from happy. When in *The Last Battle*, the final Narnia story, he describes arrival in heaven as 'the term is over: the holidays have begun',[8] this is not the cry of someone who hated learning. Rather it is the voice of the boy packed off to an appalling prep school in England while still grieving for his lost mother, the voice of the adolescent who loathed the bullying and hierarchical structure he found in the public school system, when for just a year he attended Malvern College. Lewis recognised how these experiences affected him, going so far as to suggest that the memory of yearning for home actually made it easier to understand living by faith.[9]

The life of faith, however, came neither easily nor early to Lewis. Although he speaks in *Surprised by Joy* of his awareness as a child and adolescent of something 'beyond' (joy, bliss, yearning, holiness), by his twenties, his Oxford training in ruthless logic (and perhaps the disillusionment of fighting in the trenches) had turned him into an atheist. But Christianity crept back to him gradually, and at first, unwelcomed. It was not until the age of 31 that:

> … I gave in and admitted that God was God and knelt and prayed: perhaps that night the most dejected and reluctant convert in all England.[10]

Even then he was not convinced by Christian orthodoxy or attracted to the trappings of religion, noting that 'I had as little wish to be in the church as in the zoo'.[11]

But ironically, it was on a journey to the zoo (Whipsnade in fact, in a motorcycle side car) that he finally became convinced that Jesus Christ was the son of God. Quite why then is not recorded, but he notes that when they set out he did not believe, but by the time they reached the zoo, he did![12]

A world of academe

Lewis spent most of his adult life in the rarefied atmosphere of
Oxford University. He had graduated with a first in Greek and
Latin Literature, Philosophy and Ancient History and then, just
as a casual further stroll, a first in English Literature. He went
on to teach English Literature at Magdalen College, staying for
29 years. It was during this time that the Inklings, a group of
writers including J. R. R. Tolkien, was formed. The authors met
weekly at the Eagle and Child public house, and it was there
that Frodo, Gandalf, Aslan and the White Witch took their first
steps into the world's imagination over the masculine cama-
raderie of warm beer and pipe smoke.

It would not be quite accurate though to depict Lewis's world
as entirely male. For many years he shared his Oxford home,
The Kilns, with a woman 25 years his senior, Janie Moore, and
her daughter Maureen. Lewis had fought alongside Mrs
Moore's son Paddy in the First World War and both had promised to look after the other's parent, should they die. On
Paddy's death, Lewis took up the promise and shared the home
with Mrs Moore until her death in 1951. Biographical debate is
hot on this topic, some claiming the relationship was more than
that of an adopted mother/son. If Lewis and Mrs Moore were
ever lovers, however, this seems to have been only in the very
early days, long before Lewis took up the Christian faith.
Certainly those who visited The Kilns perceived the relationship as that of a confirmed bachelor looked after by a
mother/housekeeper. Also sharing the house in latter years,
after retirement from the army, was Lewis's brother Warren
(otherwise known as Warnie), who had some sharp words to
say about Mrs Moore's difficult personality.

Warnie was equally dubious when American poet Joy
Davidman came on the scene. (Davidman was Joy's maiden
name and pen name. She is also known as Joy Gresham,
although by the time she met Lewis, her marriage to Bill
Gresham was pretty much over.) The story of Lewis's relationship with Joy is chronicled sufficiently accurately in the film
Shadowlands as not to need more explanation, although

perhaps it should be pointed out that in fact she had two sons, Douglas and David, both of whom remained with Lewis after her death. You will not be surprised to learn that a few other bits of dramatic licence are indulged in both Attenborough's take on Lewis's life and Disney's take on Narnia. We will come across some of them in later chapters.

It only remains to conclude this whistle-stop tour of the life of Lewis in conventional fashion, by noting that he died on 22 November 1963. He survived Joy by only three years, his health deteriorating very quickly after her death. Although by this time a well-known and loved international author, his passing went largely unnoticed, as it happened on the same day as President Kennedy's assassination.

A world changed and unchanging

So then, a world before the swinging sixties, feminism, Thatcherism, post-modernism, the fall of Communism, the rise of Islamic terrorism, before cheap air fares, colour TV, computers, email and the internet. An exploration of C. S. Lewis's writings occasionally brings you up short as you realise how much our culture has changed in that half-century or so. Occasionally, though, he shows amazing foresight. He questioned the view that new freedoms in talking about sex would actually make for better sexual relationships,[13] and was concerned at how the media could dominate people's thinking, leaving them unable to identify what they had learned as real life experience.[14]

During this course, as you look at our twenty-first-century culture through the lenses of Lewis's worldview, you may find yourself asking whether society has progressed. Lewis doubted it even then:

> I think that if you look at the present state of the world, it is pretty plain that humanity has been making some big mistakes.[15]

He pointed out that if this is so, there is no point in simply pressing on in the same direction. To make real progress, you need to turn round and start again on the right road. As a rational and educated man, he had to admit that this right road was not at all as he had expected:

> It is not transparent to reason. We could not have invented it for ourselves … It has the seemingly arbitrary and idiosyncratic character which science is slowly teaching us to put up with in this wilful universe. [16]

Lewis never doubted that it was possible to return to the right road (though he warned that the process, repentance, might not be much fun![17]). But through a life of commitment to the Christian faith, he was certain it was worth it:

> Look for Christ and you will find him, and with him everything else thrown in.[18]

Week One

Living in the shadows

To start you thinking

Enduring daylight robbery

Jesus said: 'The thief comes only to steal and kill and destroy. I have come that they might have life, and have it to the full.' (John 10:10)

Imagine a world where it is always winter. Not the picturesque winter of Disney's snowy landscapes, but one where chilblains bite your fingers and the cold earth numbs your toes, where your clothes are always damp, the skies are always grey, where there are no sunflowers or strawberries or long summer evenings, where a climate of suspicion means you avoid your neighbours, where you can't say what you think or even laugh at the absurdity of your oppression.

This is the world of Narnia as we first meet it. A world stuck in a sort of half-life. A world robbed of all that brings joy and delight.

The stealing of full personhood
I wonder if you ever feel that your life – the life you intended to lead, the full life you felt you were capable of – has been stolen from you?

If so, I wonder what you think it is that has robbed you?

Let me take a few guesses: the need to earn a living, the arrival of an unplanned child, caring for needy relatives, illness, disability, depression, lack of confidence, the selfishness or callousness of others?

Experiences such as these may well strip us of liberty or confidence, but I don't think they were what Jesus was talking about when he spoke of the thief. And here I hesitate, because I really didn't intend right at the start of this course to bring in something so contentious – but I think what Jesus was talking about was the Devil.

Bear with me here, suspend your disbelief for a few moments, and play the 'what if' game. What if there were some force perpetually intent on robbing you of the full life you were made for? What if some power out there was constantly twisting everything, feeding you lies, spoiling what is by making you yearn for what is not?

It's this idea that C. S. Lewis takes on in his great classic *The Screwtape Letters*, where a senior devil is training a junior in the subtleties of temptation. Screwtape very quickly teaches the novice Wormwood that one of his main aims is to dissuade his human 'patient' from ever considering the existence of beings such as themselves:

> If any faint suspicion … begins to arise in his mind, suggest to him a picture of something in red tights and persuade him that since he cannot believe in that … he therefore cannot believe in you.[1]

The subtlety of evil

So – what if? What if we are all part of a huge cosmic battle between good and evil? What if our world is under rebel control? Immediately, of course, dire fundamentalist or cultic conspiracy theories throw their images at us – demons lurking on the bedposts, Jewish financiers in league with a master race of lizards. As Lewis recognised, this area has always been an attraction to the lunatic fringe:

> There are two equal and opposite errors into which our race can fall about devils. One is to disbelieve in their existence. The other is to believe and to feel an excessive and unhealthy interest in them.[2]

Horror at being thought a loony can very easily drive us to the opposite extreme. But consider for a moment the middle ground – a healthy respect for the power of evil and especially for its subtleties. Consider the possibility that the main aim of this power is not to entrap us into spectacular evils (lusting after nine-year-old girls, flying planes into tower blocks) but into spectacularly little ones (an hour in front of *Who Wants to be a Millionaire?* when we could have phoned a friend, a cold glance when it could have been a smile), or into things that we don't recognise as evils at all, but are simply an absence of good.

The strength of Nothing

Screwtape describes as one of his successes a man who on his arrival in Hell realises that he spent most of his life doing neither what he *ought*, nor what he *liked*. He quotes the Book of Common Prayer's description of God as:

> … one without whom nothing is strong.[3]

And he goes on to point out:

> And Nothing is very strong: strong enough to steal away a man's best years not in sweet sins, but in a dreary flickering of the mind over it knows not what and knows not why ….'[4]

It is not necessarily the big dramatic sins that cause the most waste. As much damage can be done by vague day-dreams and half-hearted interests, by lazy bodies and inert minds.

> It does not matter how small the sins are, provided that their cumulative effect is to edge the man away from the Light and out into the Nothing. Murder is no better than cards if cards can do the trick.[5]

I don't know whether you believe in a personal devil? I'm not even sure what I believe myself! But what if there is a power at work, whether personal or abstract, whether from within or without, that is constantly trying to pull us away from the good? Forget red tights and pitchforks. Forget even the flamboyant evil of the White Witch (though it's interesting to note how even she can entrap with nothing more than a piece of Turkish Delight and a hinted reminder of sibling rivalries).

But remember the 'what if?' game. Because if you continue to play it – by listening out for those tiny devious whisperings in your brain – you will very soon discover just how subtle but also how deadly serious the influence of this power can be.

Group Session

Introduction   *3 mins*
Explaining the shape of the sessions
Agreeing group ground rules (see p. 11)

Getting to know one another   *7 mins*

Film clip 1: *Narnia* – Living in a cold world   *5 mins*
Lucy has just gone through the wardrobe into Narnia for the first time.

Brainstorm   *7 mins*
What would it be like if it was 'always winter but never Christmas'?

Note: Our present-day experience of Christmas may be one of such rampant materialism that it becomes a burden rather than a simple joy. Try and think beyond that into wartime austerity, and indeed the more simple lifestyle of ordinary people, before the late 1950s brought in the era of 'You've never had it so good.' What would it be like in those circumstances, if it were always winter and never Christmas? Even in our day, ignoring the pressures, what are the blessings that Christmas brings?

Discuss   *10 mins*
The witch has created an atmosphere of suspicion: '... even some of the trees are on her side'. Ironically though, as we watch Lucy going off with Mr Tumnus, we may well feel uncomfortable. Nowadays a child going off with a male (even a male faun) to his home is automatically seen as questionable at best and dangerous at worst. How much is our present society eroded by suspicion and lack of trust?

Reading   *1 min*
John 10:7–11.

Discuss   *10 mins*
Jesus very specifically talks of someone who wants to rob and destroy, very much like the White Witch. Belief in a personified 'destroyer', in other words, the Devil, is at a low ebb in much of today's church.

In what ways might lack of belief in a personal devil damage or strengthen the way we live our Christian life?

Discuss   *2 mins*
'You've made me feel warmer than I've felt in 100 years.' Lucy is a daughter of Eve and son of Adam – i.e. a human made in God's image.

How does Lucy show warmth and humanity to Mr Tumnus?

Reflect and share   *10 mins*
Think of one small touch of warmth and humanity from another, recently or in the past, that has made a difference to your life.

Film clip 2: *Shadowlands* – Living in the 'shadowlands'
                                                                 5 mins
C. S. Lewis, an Oxford academic, has arranged to meet Mrs Gresham, an American lady with whom he has been corresponding. He has brought along his brother Warnie for safety.

Brainstorm *5 mins*

What picture does this paint of C. S. Lewis? In what ways does this film clip imply that Lewis might be insulated from real experience and not living life to the full?

Reflect and share *7 mins*

In the film the term 'shadowlands' seems to suggest a life not fully lived, an awareness of something further never reached. It implies that the academic world of books is a narrow imitation of real life. Conversely, however, it makes it clear that Joy was drawn to Lewis in the first place by the depth of reality she found in his writings.

What does 'having life to the full' mean to you? How much does it mean breadth of experience (i.e. a wide variety of activities, interests and different experiences) and how much does it mean depth (i.e. a narrower range of activities pursued with more thoughtfulness, thoroughness or intensity)? Does being called to be a Christian disciple have any bearing on how you might view this?

Discuss *5 mins*

The term 'shadowlands', as coined by Lewis in his writings, refers to this earthly existence in contrast to the more vivid and 'real' world to come. It comes in the final Narnia story, *The Last Battle*, where the children find themselves in Aslan's country, a metaphor for Heaven and a brighter, deeper version of both earth and Narnia, the 'shadowlands' they have left behind.[6]

What difference, if any, might a belief in a future life make to our understanding of having life to the full now?

Discuss (Optional) *6 mins*

Are there any other issues from this session or issues from your reading so far that you would like to discuss?

Meditation *6 mins*

Reader 1

Jesus said: 'The thief comes only to steal and kill and destroy. I have come that they might have life and have it to the full.'

Silence *1 min*

Reader 2

In *The Screwtape Letters*, the senior devil teaches the novice to keep his human 'patient's' mind as much as possible in the past or the future, or on distant abstract matters, as a way of diverting them from the full life God intended. He explains that there are two things God wants us to attend to. The first is eternity, for that is our final destination. The second is the present moment, because, as he points out in a thought worth mulling over:

'The Present is the point at which time touches eternity.'[7]

Silence *(1 min)*

In the *Shadowlands* clip, Joy posed the question, 'Do you go around with your eyes shut?' How much are your eyes fully open to the present moment? How much have you closed your mind to matters beyond this world?

Reader 3

It is possible, says Lewis, to look back on life and realise that it has been spent neither in doing what you ought to have done, nor what you really wanted. Screwtape reminds his young apprentice of the subtle ways in which evil can rob and destroy us:

It is funny how mortals always picture us as putting things into their minds: in reality our best work is done by keeping things out … The Christians describe our Enemy as 'one without whom nothing is strong'. And Nothing is very strong: strong enough to steal away a man's best years …[8]

Silence *(1 min)*

Reader 4
Prayer

O Heavenly God become Human Man,

You came to us in the midst of our long winter of mistrust and
mismanagement.

You broke into humanity's dreary days with the bright hope of
something better.

You came to break the powers that might destroy us and give us
life to the full.

As we journey through Lent towards Easter, help us to accept
your precious Christmas gift of God with us – always.

Amen.

Silence   *(1 min)*

Read all together
Prayer

O God, the protector of all that trust in thee,
without whom nothing is strong, nothing is holy;
increase and multiply upon us thy mercy;
that, thou being our ruler and guide,
we may so pass through things temporal,
that we finally lose not the things eternal.
Amen.[9]

Silence   *(1 min)*

To take it further

Enjoying a sunlit land

The people living in darkness have seen a great light; on
those living in the land of the shadow of death a light has
dawned. (Matthew 4:16)

If the Devil is a somewhat taboo subject for logical, intelligent Christians these days, then Heaven is almost as bad. I guess this is partly because we simply can't picture it. We have rejected angels, harps, clouds and golden pavements, but are uncertain what to put in their place. And of course we can't talk about Heaven for long without referring to its counterpart, Hell – and that is perhaps the greatest taboo of all. We'll come back to Lewis's view of Hell later, but for now let's explore what he thought of Heaven.

The mysterious new world

The idea of the Shadowlands comes from the final chronicle of Narnia, *The Last Battle*, where the Narnians have gone through the door of the mysterious Stable (a sort of pre-*Doctor Who* TARDIS where the inside is bigger than the outside[10]) to find themselves in a vivid new world. They can't work out where they are – the landmarks seem the same as those of the Narnia they have just left – but somehow everything is different. Lord Digory (who had been Professor Kirke in the old English world) explains that the old Narnia, which would one day come to an end, was:

> 'only a shadow or a copy of the real Narnia which has always been here and always will be here: just as our own world, England and all, is only a shadow or a copy of something in Aslan's real world …'[11]

It's exactly what Plato taught, he mutters. Surely they learnt that at school.[12] But since I certainly wasn't taught Plato at school and the likelihood is that you weren't, a bit of background exploration is in order.

The myth of the cave

Plato, one of the greatest Greek philosophers, who lived around 400 years before the birth of Christ, tells a story called 'The Myth of the Cave'. It concerns some prisoners living deep in a cavern. They have been confined there since childhood and are shackled: all they can see is the back wall of the cave on which fall the shadows of figures passing by outside. But one day a prisoner escapes. As he climbs into the outside world he is at first dazzled, but eventually manages to make out the splendour of the people and plants and animals he sees. He realises that what he has seen on the back wall of the cave are only shadows of the reality which lies outside. But when he goes back to tell the other cave-dwellers, they don't believe him. He has surely been dazzled into madness. What they see on the cave wall must be all there is. In the end, they kill him.

The words at the beginning of this chapter come from Matthew's gospel, but it's curious to note that they originate from a much older source, the prophet Isaiah,[13] who first spoke them around the eighth century BCE – way before Plato. Matthew uses them just as Jesus begins to proclaim his great message, 'Repent, for the kingdom of heaven has come near.' And while Matthew doesn't specifically claim that Jesus himself used those words from Isaiah, Luke's gospel records Jesus very clearly quoting some others, 'He has sent me to proclaim freedom for the prisoners, and recovery of sight to the blind',[14] and linking them to his own mission.

Jesus spoke of the Kingdom of Heaven as a here-and-now thing as well as a there-and-then thing. He made it clear that he came to give 'life in abundance'[15] for this world, not just the next.

Strange, then, that there is an almost universal perception, certainly outside the Church, but frequently bolstered from within, that the life of a Christian has more to do with dreariness and conformity than freedom and fullness. Perhaps that takes us back to the 'what if?' idea of the Devil, the Father of Lies, constantly distorting and spoiling, trying to convince us there is nothing beyond the shadows.

The means of entry

It has to be said, though, that Jesus doesn't do anything to banish that perception with his oft-repeated claim that it is necessary to deny ourselves, take up our cross and lose our very self in order to find life.[16] Lewis's senior devil Screwtape understands, however, the deep paradox behind these disquieting words:

> When he talks of them losing their selves, he only means abandoning the clamour of self-will; once they have done that, he really gives them back all their personality and boasts that when they are wholly his they will be more themselves than ever …[17]

This then, Lewis asserts, is what the Kingdom of Heaven is all about – it is about 'more-ness'. When the children finally arrive in the new Narnia they discover that everything about it, even the very trees and hills, seems to have more brilliance and clarity and meaning.[18] The only entry to this new country is to take the risk of stooping through a humble and highly unlikely stable door.[19] The only entry, Jesus says, is by the highly unlikely and risky strategy of losing what we think of as our 'selves'.

It may be as difficult for us to imagine Heaven, a world beyond time and matter, as for the prisoners with their flickering shadows to believe in a world outside the cave. But perhaps it is possible to get a glimpse. For the Kingdom of Heaven once entered, says Jesus, is about discovering more-ness, life in abundance, then and now.

Week Two

Living with the beyond

To start you thinking

Sensing the spiritual

> Jesus said, 'Father, I want those you have given me to be with me where I am, and to see my glory, the glory you have given me because you loved me before the creation of the world.' (John 17:24)

Glory, joy, awe, transcendence, the numinous – not words that are bandied around too much in my everyday life, nor, I suspect, in yours. All the same, I have experienced them, and I bet you have too.

When C. S. Lewis wrote an autobiographical account of his journey towards faith, he called it *Surprised by Joy*. He was not referring to his late marriage, nor to any sense of happiness or pleasure or even aesthetic delight. For Lewis, in this context, 'joy' meant something more like a pang of wonder and longing, a sense of something *beyond* the solid matter of everyday experience.

Unexpected experiences
The things Lewis quotes as first arousing this sense in him as a child are hardly what you might expect: a toy garden made by his brother, a flowering currant bush, *Squirrel Nutkin* and

Norse myth.[1] Nevertheless, he claimed that whenever he talked of these surprising glimpses there was always someone who shared a similar experience, someone who had always thought they were alone in finding this *beyond*-ness at moments quite ordinary and unexpected.

It is the same experience, says Lewis, as that described by Wordsworth in his 'Lines composed above Tintern Abbey':

> ... a sense sublime
> of something far more deeply interfused.[2]

He also relates it to the feelings of Ratty and Mole in *The Wind in the Willows* when they meet the 'Piper at the Gates of Dawn':

> Then suddenly Mole felt a great Awe fall upon him, an awe that turned his muscles to water, bowed his head and rooted his feet to the ground. It was no panic terror – indeed he felt wonderfully at peace and happy – but it was an awe that smote and held him and, without seeing, he knew it could only mean that some august Presence was very, very near.[3]

A more contemporary example, that Lewis obviously didn't refer to, can be found in the film *American Beauty*, where one of the characters uses video to capture a plastic bag being blown by the wind:

> It was one of those days when it's a minute away from snowing. And there's this electricity in the air, you can almost hear it, right? And this bag was just ... dancing with me. Like a little kid begging me to play with it. For fifteen minutes. That's the day I realised that there was this entire life behind things and this incredibly benevolent force that wanted me to know there was no reason to be afraid. Ever.[4]

For Lewis this sense of what he calls the Numinous – the presence of something divine – is to be found in all peoples at all times. It is an experience that was present in the most primitive of peoples and cannot be eliminated even by the most sophisticated and learned of civilisations.[5]

Indefinable memories

I'm aware that for some people all this talk of a 'sense of beyond' will be somewhat irritating. Isn't it all a bit 'touchy-feely' and vague, unable to be defined or explained by logic? Well yes, of course, because we are talking of a sense of something outside time and therefore way beyond our understanding. We are talking of a yearning for something that cannot be fully experienced by our physical senses or understood by our finite brains. Lewis even suggests that it may be a yearning not just for something in the future, but a memory – a faint reminder from before the point when we entered time, a recollection of a 'home' we once knew. Every experience of joy, says Lewis, carries within itself:

> ... a desire for something longer ago or further away or still 'about to be'.[6]

It is this same sense of something both before and after human experience that Jesus was talking about when he prayed that his followers might one day share glory with him. 'Before' and 'after' are, of course, nonsensical expressions in this context and that is where the problem lies. We find it hard to imagine anything that does not begin or end and can see time only as a line travelling in one direction, whereas God exists in dimensions we can barely even begin to imagine.[7]

Unexplainable yearnings

But perhaps there are good reasons why we cannot understand. Perhaps we were never meant to. A Scottish character in Lewis's novel *The Great Divorce* suggests that mere mortals can never hope to see beyond the confines of time:

> Time is the very lens through which ye see ... something that would otherwise be too big for you to see at all. That thing is Freedom: the gift whereby you most resemble your Maker ... For every attempt to see the shape of

eternity except through the lens of Time, destroys your
knowledge of Freedom.[8]

We were made to live in time in order to exercise freedom, to
make choices and decisions and deal with the consequences as
things unfold one after another. So there is a reason why an
understanding of eternity has not been given us. But equally
there is a reason why a yearning for it has. When we find within ourselves a dissatisfaction that cannot be quelled, it may not
be as dysfunctional as we fear. Rather it may be quite natural
evidence that we have a further destination.

> Probably earthly pleasures were never meant to satisfy
> [desire], but only to arouse it, to suggest the real thing ...
> I must keep alive in myself the desire for my true country,
> which I shall not find until after my death.[9]

Group session

Introduction   1 min
Review ground rules. Are there any issues arising from the last
two chapters that you would like to discuss later?

Film clip 1: *Shadowlands* – Living with the unattainable
                                                                5 mins
The beginning of the film introduces Lewis with his students
and university colleagues.

Brainstorm   5 mins
What moments have you had in your life that you would
describe as magical?

Reflect and share   10 mins
Have you ever had any experiences, 'magical' or otherwise, that
you would describe as spiritual, transcendent, supernatural,
giving you a sense of something 'beyond' normal everyday
life? If so, what impact have they had on that everyday life?

Discuss *5 mins*

Lewis tells his students that: 'The most intense joy lies not in the having but in the desiring.' Would you describe this as your experience? Is it true therefore, that to travel hopefully is better than to arrive? If so, why? Is this just a view of cynicism and disillusionment, or is there more to it than that?

Reading *1 min*

Matthew 6:19–21, 25, 33.

Discuss *5 mins*

Do you find it hard to think in terms of 'storing up treasure in heaven'? If so, why?

Film clip 2: *Narnia* **– Living with the unbelievable** *5 mins*

Lucy and Edmund have just returned from her second and his first trip through the wardrobe to Narnia.

Discuss *3 mins*

Why do you think Edmund denied his experience of Narnia?

Discuss *10 mins*

Have you ever found it difficult to share your beliefs or your spiritual experience with others? When you have ventured to try to explain them, how have others reacted? If you have chosen not to share them, what were your reasons?

Brainstorm *5 mins*

List aspects of Christian belief that you find difficult to reconcile with a contemporary 'logical' or 'scientific' worldview. Then decide for each one whether it is because they seem or are illogical, because they are too hard to understand or explain, or because they are simply unfashionable.

Reflect and share *10 mins*

If you were asked what makes you most convinced of a spiritual dimension to life (something or someone 'out there' beyond what you can see or prove), how would you answer?

Discuss (Optional)   *5 mins*
C. S. Lewis questions how many people abandon their faith because they have been convinced by reasoned debate. He suggests it is rarely as logical or decisive as that.[10]

What do you think are the things most responsible for people leaving the Christian faith – painful experience, hurt feelings, or the inability to reconcile faith with reason? Can you think of any other factors?

Discuss (Optional)   *10 mins*
Any other issues arising from the course so far.

Meditation   *10 mins*

Reader 1
This life has frequently been compared with a journey to a far country. This explains, says C. S. Lewis, the restlessness we often feel:

> The settled happiness and security which we all desire, God withholds from us by the very nature of the world: but joy, pleasure and merriment, he has scattered broadcast. We are never safe but we have plenty of fun, and some ecstasy. It is not hard to see why. The security we crave would teach us to rest our hearts in this world and pose an obstacle to our return to God. A few moments of happy love, a landscape, a symphony, a merry meeting with our friends, a bathe or a football match have no such tendency. Our Father refreshes us on the journey with some pleasant inns, but will not encourage us to mistake them for home.[11]

Silence   *(1 min)*

Reader 2
Jesus said:

> 'Do not store up for yourselves treasure on earth, where
> moth and rust destroy, and where thieves break in and
> steal. But store up for yourselves treasures in heaven,
> where moth and rust do not destroy and where thieves do
> not break in and steal. For where your treasure is, there
> will your heart be also … But seek first his kingdom and
> his righteousness and all these things will be given to you
> as well.'[12]

Silence   *(1 min)*

Reader 3
Augustine of Hippo, a fifth-century bishop, said:

> You have made us for yourself, and our heart is restless
> until it finds its rest in you.[13]

Silence   *(1 min)*

Reader 4
In the final Narnia story, the characters come through the
stable door into Aslan's world, a beautiful sunlit country where
the landmarks are familiar and yet everything is different. The
Unicorn expresses what they are all feeling:

> 'I have come home at last! This is my real country! I
> belong here. This is the land I have been looking for all my
> life, though I never knew it till now. The reason why we
> loved the old Narnia is that it sometimes looked a little
> like this.'[14]

Music   *(3 mins)*
A space for quiet meditation.

Reader 4
Prayer
Lord, we are weak people bound by the constraints of time,
by faulty memory, by limited intelligence
 and a lack of observation.
There is much that we don't understand.
But sometimes we catch glimpses,
 and sometimes we find ourselves yearning
for something and someone beyond what we know.
Jesus promised the Kingdom of Heaven to those who seek it.
Lord, we are seekers. Help us to look in the right places.
Help us to trust you to bring us safely home.
Amen.

To take it further

Thinking the unthinkable

> Jesus said: 'Do not be afraid of those who kill the body but cannot kill the soul. Rather, be afraid of the one who can destroy both soul and body in hell.' (Matthew 10:28)

If C. S. Lewis's idea of Heaven is of a place of 'more-ness' – somewhere deeper and more real than the world we know – then it will not surprise you to learn that his idea of Hell is the opposite – a place of less.

His fantasy novel *The Great Divorce* describes the discoveries of some lost souls who are given the chance of a bus journey from Hell to Heaven.

Hell is described as a place of dreary streets and dingy boarded-up buildings, of drizzle and endless twilight. It is a place where everything is available but nothing satisfies, a place where people move endlessly further and further away from each other, a place where people have: 'fixed faces, full not of possibilities but of impossibilities'.[15]

The self-imprisoned

It may similarly not surprise you to discover that when these lost souls arrive in Heaven – a place described as more real, more vivid and more solid that anything experienced on earth – very few of them are eager to stay.

For to live within this deeper reality means changing. It means giving up those attitudes that have fixed them to their dreary existence: self-centredness, self-pity, refusal to admit mistakes, intellectual superiority, envy, prejudice, and above all the attitude that drives all the rest – pride.

They are people who have decided, in the words of Milton in *Paradise Lost*, that it is:

> better to reign in hell, than serve in heaven.[16]

Are Heaven and Hell then, only states of mind? Not quite, according to one of Lewis's characters:

> 'Hell is a state of mind – ye never said a truer word … But Heaven is not a state of mind. Heaven is reality itself.'[17]

And he suggests that when a self-imprisoned ego comes up against a bigger, brighter and more solid reality than itself, it is likely to flee to the safety of its closed environment.

So can we take Lewis's picture of Hell as a statement of what he actually believes? Well, yes, and no. He makes it clear in his introduction that, while it has important lessons within it, this is entirely a fictional exploration. He has no intention of provoking speculation about the exact nature of the after-life – something we cannot and are not intended to know.[18]

The final divide

However, on one issue he is adamant: that there must come finally a great divide that cannot be crossed, that there must come an utterly unavoidable moment of 'either–or':

> We are not living in a world where all roads, if followed long enough, will finally meet at the centre … I do not think that all who choose wrong roads perish; but their rescue consists in being put back on the right road … Evil

can be undone, but it cannot 'develop' into good.[19]

Of course, any ideas of Hell and judgement are both un-comfortable and unfashionable, but Lewis is not one to shirk anything he thinks is integral to what the Christian faith teaches, despite what he personally might feel about it. In the introduction to *Mere Christianity* he explains that the Christian faith:

> … is what it is and was what it was long before I was born and whether I like it or not.[20]

So, following his example, I feel I must do the same. And therefore I need to ask the hard question – did the founder of the Christian religion actually believe in Hell?

And, unavoidably, it seems he did. The rest of the Bible has very little to say about Hell, but Jesus mentions it several times, and yes, it is a fearful picture, as in the parable of the sheep and the goats, where those who did nothing for those in need are told:

> 'Away from me, you that are under God's curse! Away to the eternal fire which has been prepared for the Devil and his angels!'[21]

Clearly Jesus uses Hell as a shock tactic to remind his hearers to care for others. But equally clearly it is more than a ground-less threat. He takes it seriously. (It's important to remember though that while the fire itself is described as eternal, there is no mention of an eternity of suffering. The nature of fire is to consume. What is cast in the fire is quickly destroyed.)

So here we come again to the idea that Jesus believed in a destroying force. He mentions it, if somewhat obscurely, in the verse at the beginning of this chapter:

> '… be afraid of the one who can destroy both body and soul in hell.'

Whether this 'one' is the Devil or our own selves, Jesus does not make clear and I will leave you to ponder. But destruction, Jesus seems to say, is possible.

The triumph of joy

Certainly, Jesus teaches far more about a loving, welcoming, forgiving God than about hellfire and damnation. But we cannot erase the latter from the gospels. And so as always the juxtaposition of the two ideas immediately provokes questions: How could a loving God allow anyone to be lost? And how could anyone be happy in Heaven, knowing that anyone they loved on earth was lost? In *The Great Divorce* Lewis faces the question as to how those in Heaven can be fully joyful while even one soul remains in Hell. It sounds callous, but consider, says Lewis, who would hold the power in this scenario and what implication lies behind it:

> 'The demand of the loveless and self-imprisoned that they should be allowed to blackmail the universe: that till they consent to be happy (on their own terms) no one else shall taste joy …'[22]

Good cannot be held to ransom by evil. It must in the end be resolved:

> 'Either the day must come when joy prevails and the makers of misery are no longer able to infect it: or else for ever and ever the makers of misery can destroy in others the happiness they reject for themselves …'[23]

So, Heaven or Hell? We can picture neither and we are given very few clues. But what we are given, in the teachings of Jesus (and explored in the writings of Lewis), are some very strong promises that this life is not all there is. And some even stronger warnings that what happens in this mysterious afterwards very much depends on how we live now.

Thankfully it is not all down to some sort of good deeds/right attitudes 'score-card' or none of us would make it. There is, as we will see in next week's session, a 'deeper magic' at work.

Week Three

Living with the unexplained

To start you thinking

Facing up to suffering

'Neither this man nor his parents sinned,' said Jesus, 'but this happened so that the work of God might be displayed in his life.' (John 9:1–3)

Jesus' answer to those who questioned him on the reason for a man's blindness seems at first glance a little cold and dispassionate. Was the man born blind, then, just to be on hand when Jesus wanted to perform an impressive miracle? Was it as arbitrary as that?

It's a perennial question – why suffering? Why does a so-called loving God allow such terrible things to happen to good people? Could suffering have any possible purpose? And if so, what could it be?

The pitfalls of attempting answers

It's a brave person who attempts to give any answers to such difficult questions, but C. S. Lewis was nothing if not up for a challenge. When at the height of the Second World War he was asked to write a book on 'the problem of pain', his first thought was to write it anonymously, realising that anyone who tried to justify suffering was going to appear very cruel and become very unpopular.[1]

He made clear it that he was only tackling the intellectual problems of suffering, not the experience of it, admitting that when it came to it he was a 'great coward',[2] and that these were not just his own thoughts but ideas put forward throughout the history of the Church.

Lewis went on in later years to write a much more personal and less detached account of suffering in *A Grief Observed*, written after Joy Gresham's death (and we will look at this more in Week 5). But even before he wrote a word on these issues, he was no stranger to the problem of pain. His mother had died when he was only nine years old, and as a young man he had lost his best friend in the trenches of the First World War and been seriously wounded himself. Yet despite these experiences, he still believed that God allowed pain for a purpose.

The possibility of 'unkind' love

In *The Problem of Pain*, Lewis tackles head on the frequent assumptions that if God were all-loving he would want all people to be happy and if God were all-powerful he could alleviate pain as he wished. On the first assumption he writes:

> Love is something more stern and splendid than mere kindness ... Kindness, merely as such, cares not whether its object becomes good or bad, provided only that it escape suffering ...'[3]

But the deepest love is far more than that. A true lover wants something more for the object of their love – that they are given the opportunity to be most fully themselves.

In his most angry moments after Joy's death, Lewis compared God to a cruel vivisectionist. But later he changed the comparison to that of a surgeon intent on bringing healing and wholeness:

> The kinder and more conscientious he is, the more he will go on cutting. If he yielded to your entreaties, if he stopped before the operation was complete, all pain up to that point would have been useless ...'[4]

The unpalatable medicine of punishment

Surely Lewis doesn't believe that pain is willed on a particular individual who needs to improve? Distasteful as you or I might find that idea, Lewis, who is always prepared to think rigorously and take the Bible seriously, doesn't entirely rule it out. In correspondence with a friend he points out that while the book of Revelation and some Old Testament passages imply that suffering can be sent as a punishment, the book of Job and the gospel of John make it clear that it is not *always* that:

> It would certainly be most dangerous to assume that any given pain was penal. I believe that all pain is contrary to God's will, absolutely but not relatively.[5]

He goes on to give the example of taking a thorn from his finger. He *absolutely* does not want the pain. But *relative* to the possibility of a septic finger, the pain of removal is preferable. He also uses the example of a mother smacking a son (unacceptable now, but taken for granted then). Any loving mother would rather spare her child suffering. But equally any truly loving mother would rather discipline her child than allow him to grow up cruel or out of control.

Lewis acknowledges that he would rather 'crawl through sewers' than suffer pain. But still he explores the possibility that suffering could have a purpose:

> I am only trying to show that the old Christian doctrine of being made 'perfect through suffering' is not incredible. To prove it palatable is beyond my design.[6]

My first reaction is that it certainly is unpalatable! So I'm relieved to see that Jesus makes clear and Lewis acknowledges that serving such an idea up as a diagnosis is highly dangerous. We are not in a position to make definitive judgements on why suffering comes to any individuals – ourselves or others.

The precious ability to choose

But that doesn't mean that we can make no link between suffering and wrongdoing, simply that we must take a much bigger view in order to grasp it. And here the second assumption mentioned earlier – that God, if he so wished, could turn away suffering from those who don't deserve it – must be challenged.

The consequence of God giving humans free will – the precious ability to choose – is that good and bad must be freely available. For how could you make any significant choice if there were no significant options? And if bad options are available then people will take them – deliberately or carelessly – and that inevitably means pain and suffering for others. Often it means suffering for others far away and completely unknown – like the teenager in a Chinese sweat shop who made my cheap jeans.

The problem of untamed nature

So humans do bad things and the innocent suffer – that we can understand. Far less easy are the sufferings brought on by natural causes – plague, earthquakes, tsunamis. Lewis argues that even an all-powerful God could not create a world where humans could have free choice, without creating a natural world which offered both good and bad outcomes. He cites the example of fire: essential to life and comforting in many circumstances but lethal in others. We are grateful for the ability of our nerve endings to distinguish between warm, hot and scorching, when it provokes us to withdraw our hand from the flame.[7] If this is the case then pain must be a necessary part of life, and when it warns us of danger, something to be welcomed. In the same way, perhaps suffering which forces us to turn to God in desperation, or evokes in us reactions of love, compassion or practical action, is also to be welcomed rather than feared. As Jesus suggested, these things can have a good purpose far beyond what we might first imagine.

Having said that, I realise just how glib it all sounds and just how huge and complex a subject I have attempted to address in a ridiculously short chapter. Of course, there are times when no answers will satisfy, when it all seems far beyond understanding or explanation (and again we will return to this in Week 5).

But then again, try to picture human existence without pain, and you may find it equally difficult. Maybe, as Lewis suggests, for us to be fully human and not automatons, it is the only way it could be:

> Perhaps this is not the 'best of all possible universes' but the only possible one.[8]

Group session

Introduction   *1 min*
Share any thoughts arising from previous readings that you would like to explore. Deal with them now or note them for discussion later in the session if appropriate.

Film clip 1: *Shadowlands* **– The purpose of suffering** *3 mins*
Lewis gives a lecture on suffering, based on his book *The Problem of Pain*.

Brainstorm   *8 mins*
'What if the answer is yes?' Could Lewis be right? Could God possibly want us to suffer? Put aside for the moment the personal reactions this idea provokes in you, and brainstorm as many circumstances as possible in which pain and suffering might be a good thing?

Reflect and share   *8 mins*
In his introduction to *The Problem of Pain*, Lewis suggests:

> Reflect for five minutes on the fact that all the great religions were first preached and long practised in a world without chloroform.[9]

What thoughts does this provoke in you about human capacity for belief in God? Do you think our contemporary 'civilised' world is less willing to accept suffering than previous generations?

And/or

Reflect and share   *10 mins*

> The blows of his chisel which hurt us so much are what
> make us perfect.

Can you think of any painful experience in your life which has
helped you to grow and learn? Share it if you feel able.

Discuss   *5 mins*

> Pain is God's megaphone to rouse a deaf world.[10]

But it is still possible to close our ears. Do you ever shut out
information about suffering and if so, why? Is it ever valid to
do so?

Read   *1 min*
John 9:1–6.

Discuss   *5 mins*

> 'Who sinned, this man or his parents, that he was born
> blind?'

Is it inevitable that the sins of the fathers are visited on their
children? If so, is it fair?

Discuss   *5 mins*

> 'He was born blind so that God's power might be seen at
> work ...'

The obvious implication from this is that the man had to
remain blind until Jesus' power came along to heal him. But
do you think that is all Jesus meant? In what ways might
God's power have been at work in the man before Jesus came
along?

Discuss (Optional)   *10 mins*
Are there any other issues arising from previous readings or the session so far that you would like to discuss?

Film clip 2: *Narnia* **– The purpose of sacrifice**   *8 mins*
The White Witch has confronted Aslan, telling him that according to their laws, the traitor, Edmund, must die. After talking in private, Aslan emerges and announces that 'she has renounced her claim on the son of Adam'. That night Lucy and Susan wake to see Aslan padding off and decide to follow.

Brainstorm   *5 mins*
What similarities did you notice between this episode of Aslan's death (and what you know of what precedes and follows it) and the story of the death of Jesus in the gospels?

Discuss   *5 mins*
A quick overview of our tumultuous, suffering world might lead us to conclude that Jesus' sacrifice was in vain. Did it change anything at all? And if so, what?

Reflect and share   *8 mins*
What difference, if any, does the idea of a suffering Saviour make to your view of the sufferings you experience?

Meditation   *6 mins*
Reader 1
Jesus explains that his mission to bring life in its fullness came with a terrifying price tag:

> 'The thief comes only in order to steal, kill and destroy. I have come in order that you might have life – life in all its fullness. I am the good shepherd, who is willing to die for the sheep … No one takes my life away from me. I give it up of my own free will. I have the right to give it up and I have the right to take it back. This is what my Father has commanded me to do.'[11]

Silence   *(1 min)*

Reader 2

C. S. Lewis explains that a truly loving God is far more awesome than we often realise:

> You asked for a loving God: you have one. The great spirit you so lightly invoked [is] not a senile benevolence that drowsily wishes you could be happy in your own way, not the cold philanthropy of a conscientious magistrate, nor the care of a host who feels responsible for the comfort of his guests, but the consuming fire himself, the Love that made the worlds, persistent as the artist's love for his work … and venerable as a father's love for a child …[12]

Music   *(3 mins)*

A space for quiet reflection on the enormity of God's love.

Reader 3
Prayer

Lord, we would rather have a world without suffering,
    than a world with compassion.
We would rather you set limits to evil,
    than allow us full responsibility.
We would rather you let us 'get away with it',
    than challenged us to be better.
We prefer comfort to goodness; tolerance to stringent love.
We want life in its fullness – and sometimes we don't consider
    or care what that costs others.

Lord, we don't understand why you made the world the way
    you did,
but if pain is part of the package,
    then strengthen us to accept it.
If suffering seems incomprehensible,
    then help us to trust where we do not understand.

If your will is not always pleasant to us,
    then teach us to say 'Thy will be done.'

Silence   *(1 min)*

To take it further

Finding the deeper magic

> For all have sinned and fall short of the glory of God, and
> are justified freely by his grace through the redemption
> that came by Christ Jesus. (Romans 3:23–24)

I don't know about you, but as I've delved into this idea of
suffering, I've begun to see at least a few gleams of logic:

- to be human means consciousness, conscience and the need
  to make moral choices;
- to make those choices demands the availability of both good
  and evil options;
- the availability of evil means that innocent people suffer.

So far, so good. A host of questions still unanswered, but at
least a few germs of understanding of why the world is as it is.

But if I ask why the Christian religion is as it is, it's a different story. Why does it all revolve around one man and his
death? Why this arbitrary point in history? What did it really
achieve? Does it really make a difference?

Well, yes. When I'm facing hard things, it certainly helps
that the Christian religion holds suffering at its heart as well. It
helps that it offers not a remote austere God but a father in
anguish because his son is in pain. It helps that it centres on an
innocent man taking the blame for others.

But is that the only meaning of the death of Jesus – something for us to identify with, a sort of metaphor to help us latch
on to the idea of a loving God?

Well, no. The Christian religion claims that this one man at this one point in history did much more than illuminate the idea of a loving God for us. It claims that he actually became the way for us to reach God. It claims that this one sacrifice actually takes on all the blame and punishment that we should otherwise suffer, and frees us to enter into the presence of a perfect holy God, free from blemish. It claims that through this one act, we can be born again.

And that – if you are one of those people like me, who always has to question everything – can sometimes seem very odd.

How odd of God

One of the things I love about C. S. Lewis is his acknowledgement that the Christian religion is indeed very odd. He memorably compares this new spiritual birth to our physical human birth and the sexual act that preceded it. He describes the latter as:

> … a very curious process, involving pleasure, pain and danger. A process you would never have guessed. Most of us spend a good many years in our childhood trying to guess it: and some children when they are first told, do not believe it – and I am not sure that I blame them, for it is very odd.[13]

Often familiarity with these processes – be it sex and a human baby, or Jesus' sacrifice and spiritual rebirth – make us forget how odd they are. Particularly as seasoned Christians, it is easy to forget how strange these ideas like sacrifice and redemption are for people who first encounter them. Although for Lewis it was this very oddity that in the end convinced him of Christianity:

> It is a religion you could not have guessed … It is not the sort of thing anyone would have made up.[14]

Complexity and simplicity

And he claims that besides this oddity, its very complexity also makes it believable. A simple religion is a tempting proposition, but it could never be authentic, because it has to take on the real world – and real life is an unbelievably complex affair.

Look closely at anything in the material world, and you discover how even the apparently most uncomplicated of things is not simple at all. Lewis cites the example of the table where he sits. It looks simple. It looks solid, but in fact if you examine it at atomic level, it is mostly made up of empty space. It looks still, but if you think about it at the sub-atomic level, it is made up of raw jangling energy.[15]

A religion that takes on the complications of the real world must be complex too. It is no good asking to understand it fully. As Lewis points out, even the best explanations the scientists can give us of the structure of the material world are nothing but pictures, metaphors if you like, of something that can only truly be expressed mathematically. And so it is with faith, we can only see glimpses, pictures (shadows even) of a real thing that even the wisest theologians can never fully express:

> If we cannot picture even the atoms of which our own world is built, of course we are not going to be able to picture this.[16]

Theory and practicality

Fortunately, I don't need to understand the molecular physics of the table to trust it to hold my laptop as I sit and write this. And fortunately for me, I don't need to understand difficult theological concepts – incarnation, atonement, redemption – in order to experience them. As Lewis writes:

> A good many different theories have been held as to how it works; what all Christians are agreed on is that it does work.[17]

I agree. It does work. I may not be able to give a logical explanation, but over the years I've learned that when I offer up the day-by-day struggles and heartaches of life in prayer, then day-by-day I experience small redemptions that bring good out of bad things. I've learned that living by the wisdom of this odd carpenter Messiah brings constant small rebirths that put me on my feet and set me on the right path.

And so, I've learned to believe that, as Aslan explained in *The Lion, the Witch and the Wardrobe*, there is a 'deeper magic' at work.[18] The Christian world calls it 'grace' – and the great thing is that you don't need to understand it to experience it.

Week Four

Living with what we've been given

To start you thinking

Maximising our potential

> Jesus said: 'Come to me, all you who are weary and burdened, and I will give you rest. Take my yoke upon you and learn from me for I am gentle and humble in heart, and you will find rest for your souls. For my yoke is easy and my burden is light.' (Matthew 11:29–30)

My generation, the baby boomers, has been given a life much softer than that which Lewis experienced. As a young man he fought in the trenches of the First World War; in middle-age he experienced the privations and difficulties of the Second.

No wonder then that when he came to writing *The Lion, the Witch and the Wardrobe*, it centred around a battle. In fact, the initial inspiration probably came from the evacuee children who stayed in his Oxford home during the early years of the war.

A bracing worldview

The wartime world was one in which everyone had to do their bit. Chickens were kept in the Lewis's garden. Vegetables were grown, even though the gardener was sent to work at the munitions factory. Lewis himself, by then too old to fight, contributed by using the gifts he had. They were gifts unique to him – the ability to make sense of pain and suffering, the ability to bring spiritual meaning to the complex experiences of battle. He wrote his first Christian book, *The Problem of Pain*, in 1939. He spent much time visiting RAF bases where he gave stirring talks on Christian themes. And then in 1941 he was asked by the BBC to give a series of broadcasts on spiritual topics, which later went on to become the great Christian classic, *Mere Christianity*.

So it is also no wonder, given the slice of history that Lewis inhabited, that his worldview is somewhat more bracing, more uncompromising, more determined than ours. Death hovered much more closely, therefore life became a much more serious matter.

And when Lewis studied his Bible, there too he found the same uncompromising seriousness of purpose. He describes what he thinks a truly Christian society would look like, as drawn from the hints he finds in the New Testament:

> Everyone is to work with his own hands and what is more, everyone's work is to produce something good: there will be no manufacture of silly luxuries and then of sillier advertisements to persuade us to buy them.[1]

Whatever would he have made of twenty-first-century shopping malls and TV ads?

But while on the one hand he sees New Testament living as socialist, on the other he sees its insistence on obedience – children to parents, wives to husbands and citizens to their legal rulers – as something many would regard as reactionary and right wing.[2]

An uncompromising gospel

This is the problem with Christianity, he observes, that everyone is attracted to some parts but wants to pick out those bits and leave the rest. Indeed even as he writes he is aware that there are some things he would rather leave out.[3]

In *Mere Christianity*, Lewis heads one of his chapters with a question: 'Is Christianity hard or easy?' He points out that many of us think when we become Christians we will just have to put right a few glaring faults and that will be it – we will be free to continue life as we choose. Thinking that way is no good at all, says Lewis:

> In the end you will either give up trying to be good, or else become one of those people who, as they say, 'live for others' but always in a discontented, grumbling way ... always making a martyr of yourself. And once you have become that you will be a far greater pest ... than you would have been if you had remained frankly selfish ... The Christian way is different: harder and easier. Christ says 'Give me your all.' [4]

So compromise is out. Christianity, as Jesus sometimes outlines it, seems an impossible choice. After all, doesn't he even demand 'Be perfect ... as your heavenly Father is perfect'?[5] What can he possibly mean? Lewis has a theory:

> When he said 'Be perfect' he meant it. He meant that we must go in for the full treatment. It is hard, but the sort of compromise we are hankering after is harder – in fact, it is impossible. It may be hard for an egg to turn into a bird: it would be a jolly sight harder for it to learn to fly while remaining an egg.[6]

Jesus takes this tough and idealistic line because he wants us to become what we were intended to be. He wants us to unleash our potential. He wants us to be fully ourselves.

The curious thing about Jesus is that sometimes he describes the Christian way as very easy and at other times as very hard. He means both, says Lewis. In the verse at the beginning of this chapter, Jesus offers rest. But he offers it by also offering work: 'Take my yoke upon you.' Become like the oxen pulling the plough. When we pull in directions we were never intended to go, we become weary and burdened. When we go where he leads, even though we work hard, our spirits are rested. And here is the paradox – when we are most fully under his command, we become most fully ourselves.

Group session

Introduction
Are there any issues arising from previous readings that anyone
would like to discuss later?

Film Clip 1: *Narnia* **– The gift of a purpose**   *5 mins*
The children meet Father Christmas.

Discuss   *8 mins*

    'They are tools, not toys.'

Do today's children get too many toys or too much amusement?
What dangers might lie behind all this bounty? Do you think
there is something wrong with our attitude to childhood? If so,
what?

Reflect and share   *8 mins*
Have you ever been given a really good gift (material or spiritual) – one which has gone on enhancing your life rather than
just giving temporary pleasure? What was special about it?

Brainstorm   *10 mins*
List the worst-case scenarios that we or our children might face
during the next 50 years.
    List ways in which we or they might be better equipped –
spiritually, mentally or physically – to face these challenges.

Read   *1 min*
Matthew 7:7–11: God's good gifts.

Discuss   *5 mins*
Can we treat God like Father Christmas, bringing a wish list of
things we want to have? Or should we expect him to deal only

in needs?

Film Clip 2: *Shadowlands* – The gift of the present moment

4 mins

When Joy's illness goes into remission, she and Lewis visit the Golden Valley. As a child Lewis had a painting of this place on his wall. He always identified it with Heaven.

Discuss

8 mins

'The pain then is part of the happiness now. That's the deal.'

What do you think this statement means and do you agree with it?

Discuss

4 mins

Back in the Old Testament, Job asks a penetrating and fundamental question: 'Shall we accept good from God and not trouble?'[7]

What would your answer be?

Reflect and share

8 mins

Have you ever had an experience where pain and happiness (or joy) have gone hand in hand? Share it if you feel able.

Read

1 min

Philippians 4:10–13: the secret of contentment.

Discuss

3 mins

Is this sense of contentment the same as that expressed by Lewis in the film? If not, what is different?

Reflect and share

8 mins

In the film, Lewis says he is '... not looking for anything else to happen, not wanting to be anywhere else. Here, now, that's enough.'

Do you ever feel this sense of contentment, or that which Paul speaks of in Philippians? If so, how do you think you acquired or learned it?

Discuss (Optional)   *4 mins*
Are there any issues arising from this week's session or previous readings that you would like to discuss?

Meditation   *10 mins*
Reader 1
This is the same passage as that we read earlier, only this time from Luke's gospel. Listen out for the difference – the very specific gift offered at the end:

> 'Ask and it will be given to you; seek and you will find; knock and the door will be opened to you … Which of you fathers if your son asks for a fish will give him a snake instead? … If you then, though you are evil, know how to give good gifts to your children, how much more will your Father in heaven give the Holy Spirit to those who ask him!'[8]

Silence   *(1 min)*

Reader 2
In this passage, from one of C. S. Lewis's science fiction novels *Perelandra* (also known as *Voyage to Venus*), the Lady, a sort of Eve figure on an unspoilt planet, learns that it is possible to ruin what you have by yearning after what you cannot have:

> 'One goes into the forest to pick food and already the thought of one fruit rather than another has grown up in one's mind. Then, it may be, one finds a different fruit and not the fruit one thought of. One joy was expected and another is given. But this I had never noticed before – that at the very moment of the finding, there is in the mind a kind of thrusting back or setting aside. The picture of the

fruit you have not found is still, for a moment, before you. And if you wished – if it were possible to wish – you could keep it there. You could send your soul after the good you had expected, instead of turning to the good you had got. You could refuse the real good; you could make the real fruit taste insipid by thinking of the other.'[9]

Silence   *(1 min)*

Music   *(3 mins)*

Reader 4
Prayer

Lord, sometimes we are so busy
    demanding what we think we need
that we do not notice what we have already been given.
Sometimes we are so preoccupied
    with complaints about the rain
that we fail to look up and see the rainbow.
We focus on the pain and miss the laughter,
concentrate on the discomfort and overlook the loving care,
get frustrated with what we cannot do
    and fail to do what we can.

Or, Lord, we do the opposite.
We get so used to comfort
    that we forget that we will also discover you amid the hurt.
We get so used to pleasure
    that we don't believe we could possibly meet you in the pain.

Lord, help us to look for you in all our life's experiences.
Help us to build the life you destined us for,
    by using the gifts you have given.

Silence   *(1 min)*

To take it further

Accepting ups and downs

Job said: 'Shall we accept good from God and not trouble?' (Job 2:10)

Paul said: 'I have learned the secret of being content in any and every situation ...' (Philippians 4:12)

I was on holiday in France many years ago when I first read the passage from *Perelandra* quoted in this week's meditation (p. 60–1). The trouble was, I was supposed to be on holiday in Portugal. A group of us had gone across the channel with an old minibus and the intention to travel right down through Europe to visit a Christian group in Porto. Unfortunately, the minibus broke down on the first day. It soon became clear that it wouldn't be fixed in a hurry. (In fact, it finally came back in pieces on the back of a lorry many weeks later.) The insurance we thought covered us turned out to have a loophole that did not cover us fully at all. There was no hiring another vehicle. So, stowing our camping gear in the guards van, we took a train to the nearest seaside, which was, everyone assured us, 'très jolie'. Our luggage got lost. The campsite turned out to be between a trunk road and a mainline railway. The sea was far out beyond pebbles and a quarter mile of mud. We got sunburnt. We had diarrhoea. And so on ...

But when many of us look back on it years later, we all agree it was one of the best holidays we ever had! We hired cycles, ate seafood, took a boat-trip and above all just hung around the tents and laughed together! And I learned in the most vivid way possible to appreciate the fruit I had and not to hanker after the fruit that was out of reach. Over thirty years later I'm still thankful for that disastrous holiday.

A struggling saint

I certainly can't claim that insight has calmed all restlessness and frustration since. But perhaps such super-spiritual serenity is only the property of saints? Well, it has to be said that a further reading of the New Testament doesn't reveal St Paul as the cheery laid-back type:

> What I do is not the good I want to do.[10]

> What a wretched man I am.[11]

> They [Paul and Barnabas] had such a sharp disagreement that they parted company.[12]

> There was given me a thorn in my flesh, a messenger of Satan to torment me.[13]

> I am afraid that when I come I may not find you as I want you to be and you may not find me as you want me to be.[14]

No, Paul had the same ups and downs as the rest of us. The 'secret of being content' that he claims in Philippians seems to have less to do with a euphoric state of delight than a hard-learned willingness to accept what comes. Lewis too seems to have learned this acceptance of 'ups and downs' as the unavoidable stuff of life:

> One never meets just Cancer or War or Unhappiness (or Happiness). One only meets each hour or moment that comes. All manner of ups and downs. Many bad spots at our best times, many good ones at our worst.[15]

He wrote those words shortly after the death of Joy Gresham, explaining how this understanding disarmed much of the fear they had felt at the 'C word' diagnosis. He went on to describe how precious the good times were among the bad:

> It is incredible how much happiness, even how much gaiety, we sometimes had together after all hope was gone.

How long, how tranquilly, how nourishingly, we talked together that last night.[16]

An undulating landscape

But Lewis goes further than merely accepting 'ups and downs' as the interwoven stuff of life. He claims they are a vital part of God's plan. In *The Screwtape Letters*, the senior devil describes these 'undulations' as the natural state for humans to be in:

> Their nearest approach to constancy therefore is un-dulation … a series of troughs and peaks … Now it may surprise you to learn that in his [God's] efforts to get permanent possession of a soul, he relies on the troughs even more than the peaks; some of his special favourites have gone through longer and deeper troughs than anyone else.[17]

In that case it makes sense to do as St Paul suggests:

> Give thanks in all circumstances, for this is God's will for you in Christ Jesus.[18]

We all know it's not as simple as it sounds, and a dangerously glib piece of advice to give to anyone whose life has been one long round of trouble. We are weak, fragile creatures, every one of us, and we cannot assume that triumph is inevitable. We all have our breaking point. But giving thanks for our circum-stances, whatever they are, does seem to have been throughout history a good recipe for survival, if not always triumph. Commenting on the Psalms, those gloriously realistic ancient poems, Lewis (with an equally realistic proviso that sometimes an appalling situation makes thanksgiving impossible), suggests that:

> Praise almost seems to be inner health made audible.[19]

I have to say that I've been in some worship services where endless trite praise songs have seemed more like inner denial made audible! That aside, I would endorse Lewis's observation that when it comes to real gratitude and delight, it is more often seen in those who are most balanced and down to earth.[20]

It seems that those who've genuinely learned this lesson –
the psalmists, St Paul, Lewis – have wisdom worth following.
They've learned that praise sometimes comes through gritted
teeth. They know that it's OK to allow our anger, frustration
and grief to land on God's broad shoulders. They understand
that we must be real, and that out of that acknowledgement of
reality – the ups and downs, the pain and happiness inter-
mingled – then acceptance, that most wistful and wise peace,
will come.

Week Five

Living with absence

To start you thinking

Undergoing the pain

> Jesus said: 'Blessed are those who mourn …' (Matthew 5:4)

It would have been nice to start this last week on a comforting high note! But journeying with C. S. Lewis was never going to be a comfortable ride, and it would be less than honest if we didn't explore, along with Lewis, one of the most frequent experiences of spiritual journeying – that of God's absence. We can pull out biblical promises and talk about footprints in the sand, but the truth remains – sometimes it seems that God has deserted us.

I don't want to negate the experience of very many Christians of God's presence at times of grief and desperation, but there are plenty of others to attest that at their hour of greatest need they felt the most abandoned. Lewis was one of them.

A door slammed in the face
If there was ever anyone who should have been able to handle pain and suffering, it was C. S. Lewis. Author of one of the most incisive and highly-acclaimed works on the subject, high-profile advocate of faith, not even a stranger to the experience of suffering, having lost his mother at the age of nine and

fought in the Battle of the Somme. But this was grief of a new
magnitude. He had found in his sixties the happiness that had
passed him by in his twenties. 'We feasted on love,' he wrote.[1]
And when this late-blooming love was taken from him after
only three years, he crumpled like the weakest agnostic.

> Meanwhile, where is God? … Go to him when your need
> is desperate, when all other help is vain and what do you
> find? A door slammed in your face, and a sound of bolt-
> ing and double-bolting on the inside. After that, silence.[2]

Lewis chronicled this journey of bereavement in the small
volume *A Grief Observed*. Originally published under a
pseudonym, his identity was soon discovered and despite, or
perhaps because of, its unflinching honesty it became one of
his most popular works. It shows how even the most stalwart of
believers can lose all sense of trust in what they once held dear:

> The conclusion I dread is not 'So there's no God after all,'
> but 'So this is what God is really like. Deceive yourself no
> longer.'[3]

The film *Shadowlands* leaves Lewis in that state of doubt, but
his writings show a faith regained inch by inch. A few pages
further on he writes:

> Aren't all these notes the senseless writhings of a man
> who won't accept the fact there is nothing we can do with
> suffering except to suffer it? [4]

Later he begins to wonder if this sense of God's absence could
even have been something he brought on himself:

> I have gradually been coming to feel that the door is no
> longer shut and bolted. Was it my own frantic need that
> slammed it in my face? The time when there is nothing at
> all in your soul except a cry for help may be just the time
> when God can't give it: you are like the drowning man
> who can't be helped because he clutches and grabs.
> Perhaps your own reiterated cries deafen you to the voice
> you hoped to hear.[5]

He recalls how he was previously quite prepared to accept Jesus, saying: 'Blessed are those who mourn', and reminds himself:

'I've got nothing I hadn't bargained for …'[6]

A cry of despair

Jesus told his followers not only that mourners were blessed but also those who were persecuted and suffered for the Kingdom. However, even Jesus at his darkest moment exhibited anything but a sense of blessing.

'My God, my God, why have you forsaken me?'[7]

Jesus was honest enough to say it and the gospel writer was honest enough to record it. And although it perplexes me, I'm glad. Because maybe it's that moment above all that shows Jesus at his most fully human. This is what it means to be Man. We all share it and he shared it too.

Is this then the blessedness of mourning – that it takes our humanity to its greatest depths? I don't know. But I know this chapter needs to end on a reminder. Jesus said:

'Blessed are those who mourn, *for they will be comforted.*'[8]

Whether he intended it as a promise for this life or the next, I can't claim to know. But Jesus said it and he did know. He returned to show that however deep the feeling of being abandoned, it is not the end of the story. He promised that for those who follow him it never is.

Group session

Film clip 1: *Shadowlands* **– When belief is tested**   *5 mins*
After Joy's death, Lewis discovers that everything he thought he knew has been swept away.

Brainstorm   *5 mins*
When confronted with someone who has been bereaved or is
suffering, in what ways do people try and express concern and
consolation? List as many as you can, clichés and platitudes
included. Start with the reactions shown in the film and then
add others from your own experience.

Reflect and share   *10 mins*
If you have gone through a time of grief, which of the different
reactions listed in the brainstorm were most helpful? Which
was better, silence or attempts at consolation? What made the
difference?

Discuss   *5 mins*
Is it better to rail at God in the face of grief and suffering or
accept it passively and without question?

Reflect and share   *10 mins*
Have there been times in your life when the sheer hurt of some-
thing blocked out any sense of God? If so, did that sense of
God come back and if so, how?

Read   *1 min*
Matthew 27:39–50: the crucifixion of Jesus.

Discuss   *8 mins*
How do you react to the knowledge that Jesus also faced a terrifying sense of being abandoned? Does it comfort you or
alarm you?

Film clip 2: *Narnia* – When God is absent   *3 mins*
The battle is won, the witch is vanquished and the children are
made kings and queens of Narnia.

Discuss   *5 mins*
Do you think the kings and queens of Narnia would have
governed better with Aslan's presence or without it? In which

circumstance would they have learned more?

Brainstorm   *5 mins*
Why might God's 'absence' be good for us? List as many reasons as possible.

Discuss (Optional)   *10 mins*
Do you think the Church has tried to 'tame' God? If so, in which ways?

Read   *1 min*
Matthew 28:16–20: Jesus' final appearance to his disciples – and his final promise.

Discuss   *5 mins*
Does Jesus' final promise mean that we should always be aware of God's presence at those times when we most desperately need him? Can he be 'with' us even though we have no sense of his presence?

Reflect and share (Optional)   *5 mins*
In the book of *The Lion, the Witch and the Wardrobe* it is Mr Beaver, rather than Mr Tumnus, who describes Aslan as not being a tame lion, adding, 'He'll often drop in. Only you mustn't press him.'[9]

The gospel story ends with a series of unpredictable appearances by the risen Jesus.

Does the idea of a sudden unexpected meeting with Jesus frighten or excite you?

Meditation   *10 mins*

Reader 1

> Jesus said: 'The thief comes only to steal and kill and destroy. I came that they might have life and have it in abundance.'[10]

In the silence, meditate on the promise of Jesus to give us life in all its fullness. Consider the possibility that fullness encompasses grief as well as joy, pain as well as pleasure, responsibility as well as release.

Silence   *(1 min)*

Reader 2

In one of the Chronicles of Narnia, *The Silver Chair,* a schoolgirl called Jill finds herself suddenly transported to a beautiful mountain where she meets Aslan. He gives her a mission to help restore the land of Narnia. But first he tells her about some vital signs that will help her fulfil her task and sends her on her way with a warning:

> 'Here on the mountain I have spoken to you clearly. I will not often do so down in Narnia … And the signs which you have learned here will not look at all as you expect them to look when you meet them there. That is why it is so important to know them by heart and pay no attention to appearances. Remember the signs and believe the signs. Nothing else matters.'[11]

Silence   *(1 min)*

Reader 3
Prayer

O Lord, our Lord, why do you abandon us?
Do you really think we can cope with grief and pain
   and difficult demands?
Because we know we cannot.
We know we will struggle and fail and let you down
      – again and again.
We know we will turn away from you and turn against you
   and blame you
      – again and again.

Help us to remember that you also knew that was possible –
and perhaps inevitable.

And that even knowing it, you still call us to be your disciples
– to take up whatever cross we happen to be given and to
follow you.

You still offer us forgiveness and the chance to be washed
clean.

You still offer life in all its fullness because you still believe in
us and what we have the capacity to become.

Help us to trust where we cannot see.

To remember in the cloudy times what we learned in times of
clarity.

And to believe your promise that, no matter what it feels like,
you will be with us always.

Music   (3 mins)

For quiet meditation.

Leader

Lord, as we near the end of this year's Lenten journey,

renew in our memory those things that seemed to speak
especially to us.

Re-invigorate us to continue grappling with those things we
found difficult.

Remind us of those things you are calling us to put into action.

Refresh us to continue on the road in the direction you are
calling.

Together

And now may the grace of our Lord Jesus Christ,
the love of God
and the fellowship of the Holy Spirit
Be with us all now and always. Amen.

To take it further

Uncovering the purpose

> Jesus said: 'I came that they might have life and have it in abundance.' (John 10:10)

It has become a recurring theme as I have written this course: the idea that God intends us to have life in all its fullness. And it has become abundantly, if uncomfortably, clear as I have read through Lewis's works, that it was always intended for this fullness to encompass *troughs* as well as *peaks*, *pains* as well as *pleasures*, *absence* as well as *presence*. It isn't a design fault but part of the design itself!

So just as Aslan sets the children on thrones in Cair Paravel and then pads away across the sand into the sunset, so Jesus calls us to follow him and then inevitably (and often quite early on in our Christian experience) withdraws for a while and leaves us apparently to our own devices.

To stand on our own two feet
The senior devil Screwtape understood God's purpose in this:

> He is prepared to do a little overriding at the beginning ... But he never allows this state of affairs to last long. Sooner or later he withdraws, if not in fact, at least from their conscious experience, all those supports and incentives. He leaves the creature to stand up on its own legs – to carry out from the will alone duties which have lost all relish.[12]

Jesus also knew the necessity of letting his followers stand on their own two feet at the earliest opportunity:

> He called his twelve disciples to him and gave them authority to drive out evil spirits and to heal every disease and sickness ... These twelve Jesus sent out with the following instructions: 'Do not go among the Gentiles or enter any town of the Samaritans. Go rather to the lost

sheep of Israel. As you go preach this message: "The kingdom of heaven is near." Heal the sick, raise the dead,
cleanse those who have leprosy, drive out demons. Freely
you have received, freely give. Do not take along any gold
or silver or copper in your belts; take no bag for the journey, or extra tunic or sandals or a staff; for the worker is
worthy of his keep … I am sending you out like sheep
among wolves. Therefore be as shrewd as snakes and as
innocent as doves.'[13]

What a commission! What daunting tasks to leave to the likes
of impetuous Peter, doubting Thomas and the competitive Sons
of Thunder.[14] It seems God likes to set challenges.

Like Peter, Susan, Edmund and Lucy as they are crowned
kings and queens of Narnia. God takes us on as children but
wants us to become grown-ups. His intention is for us to man-
age responsibly the little bit of his kingdom he has given us. He
intends for us to rule. And for that, says C.S. Lewis:

He wants a child's heart but a grown-up's head.[15]

We need to retain a child-like nature: eager, responsive and
willing to learn, but develop a mind and body that are strong,
controlled and 'in first-class fighting trim'.

To become what we have the potential to be
It is a paradox captured perfectly in the words of George
McDonald, one of the writers who most influenced Lewis:

God is easy to please but hard to satisfy.[16]

God takes us as we are, but wants us to become more. And we
become more by exercising our wills and by making our own
free choices. And slowly these choices accumulate, if they are
good ones leading us closer to the heart of God.[17]

With God always at our side, directing operations as it were,
we might never learn this art of choice-making. The problem,
of course, is that we cannot learn without making mistakes
along the way. The great thing is that God accepts our failure.
Writing in the context of sexual chastity (a challenge Lewis

acknowledges as seemingly impossible, but claims is attainable with God's help and practice), he writes:

> Never mind. After each failure, ask forgiveness, pick your-self up and try again … The only fatal thing is to sit down content with anything less than perfection.[18]

So even at those times when we feel abandoned and the chal-lenge seems impossible – and perhaps especially at those times – what we are heading towards is life in all its fullness. It is a time that the senior devil Screwtape has learned to dread:

> Our cause is never more in danger than when a human, no more desiring, but still intending to do our enemy's will, looks round on a universe from which every trace of him seems to have vanished and asks why he has been forsak-en and still obeys.[19]

God wants us to experience *both* the precious gift of his absence *and* the precious gift of his presence (and it seems impossible to predict which comes when) in order to transform us into the holistic 'life in its fullness' people he wants us to be:

> Every now and then one meets them. Their very voices and faces are different from ours, stronger, quieter, happi-er, more radiant … They do not draw attention to them-selves. You tend to think you are being kind to them when they are being kind to you. They love you more than other men do, but they need you less … They will usually seem to have a lot of time, you will wonder where it comes from …[20]

Where does it come from, this full unhurried life? Well, of course, Lewis must have the last word and what better than the whole-hearted conviction with which he ends his classic *Mere Christianity*:

> Look for Christ and you will find him, and with him everything else thrown in.[21]

Holy Week

Meditative Service

A table in the centre or at the front should be arranged with symbols of death and rebirth:

- *Seeds*
- *Tray or pot of soil*
- *A crucifix*
- *Bare branches with just the faintest signs of green life.*

Leader

This is a time of reflection, using the words of C. S. Lewis to help us. It is a time to consider the signs of new life we see around us and to reflect again on the amazing gospel story of death and resurrection.

Death and rebirth – it is, says C. S. Lewis, a pattern that runs right through the natural and the spiritual world.

Reader 1

In the Christian story God descends to re-ascend. He comes down; down from the heights of absolute being into time and space, down into humanity. In this descent and re-ascent everyone will recognise a familiar pattern: a thing written all over the world. It is the pattern of all vegetable life. It must belittle itself into something hard, small and deathlike, it must fall into the ground: thence the new life re-ascends.[1]

Reader 2

Death and Re-birth – go down to go up – it is a key principle. Through this bottleneck, this belittlement, the highroad nearly always lies ... The pattern is there in Nature because it was first there in God.[2]

Music or Song 1 or Silence

Leader
If Jesus' death and resurrection really happened, Lewis argued, then it must be 'the central event in the history of the earth'.[3] But how could you know it was real? As an expert on literary criticism, one who had devoured myths and legends for the whole of his life, when Lewis studied the gospels he became aware that there was nothing else quite like them in the whole of literature. He was convinced that the gospel accounts had the ring of factual truth about them.[4]

Listen now to extracts of those accounts from the gospels of Mark and Matthew.

Reader 3
Mark 14:32–46: the terrified Saviour.

Reader 4
Matthew 27:33–50: the abandoned Son.

Reader 1
C. S. Lewis, commenting on the gospel story, wrote:

> God could, had he pleased, have been incarnate in a man of iron nerves, the Stoic sort who lets no sigh escape him. Of his great humility he chose to be incarnate in a man of delicate sensibilities who wept at the grave of Lazarus and sweated blood in Gethsemane.[5]

The vulnerability of Jesus shows us where true human goodness lies: that the strength that comes from acts of the will matters more than natural attributes, that feelings are ultimately unimportant, it is actions and choices that matter.

It shows us too that God fully understands us. He has faced the worst that life can throw at us, he knows what it means to be weak and at the mercy of others.

Above all he has faced the ultimate depth of the human condition, the sense of being separated from God.

Music or Song 2 or Silence

Leader
It was not, of course, the end of the story. Let us hear from the gospel accounts again, this time from John.

Reader 2
John 20:1–18: the astonished Disciples.

Leader
Did these disciples remember what Jesus had said just a few days earlier?

> 'The hour has come for the Son of Man to be glorified. Very truly, I tell you, unless a grain of wheat falls into the earth and dies, it remains just a single grain; but if it dies, it bears much fruit ... And I, when I am lifted up from the earth, will draw all people to myself.' [6]

Leader
So as Lewis summed it up, the Son of God became human to enable humans to become sons and daughters of God.[7] He took on death that death might be defeated:

> ... the really tough work – the bit we could not have done for ourselves – has been done for us. We have not got to try to climb up into spiritual life by our own efforts; it has already come down into the human race. If we will only lay ourselves open to the one Man in whom it was fully present, and who, in spite of being God, is also a real man, He will do it in us and for us.[8]

Music or Song 3 or Silence

Leader
But it doesn't quite end there. Jesus made it clear that this

pattern of death and rebirth must also run through us.

Reader 4

Jesus said:

> 'If any want to become my followers, let them deny them-
> selves and take up their cross daily and follow me. For those
> who want to save their life will lose it, and those who lose
> their life for my sake will save it. What does it profit them if
> they gain the whole world, but lose or forfeit themselves?'[9]

Reader 1

C. S. Lewis explains:

> The principle runs through life from top to bottom. Give
> up yourself and you will find your real self. Lose your life
> and you will save it. Submit to death, death of your ambi-
> tions and favourite wishes every day and death of your
> whole body in the end: submit with every fibre of your
> being and you will find eternal life. Keep nothing back.
> Nothing that you have not given away will ever really be
> yours. Nothing that has not died will ever be raised from
> the dead. Look for yourself and you will find in the long
> run only hatred, loneliness, despair, rage, ruin and decay.
> But look for Christ and you will find him and with him
> everything else thrown in.[10]

All

Lord God, Holy Father,
I am no longer my own, but yours.
Put me to what you will, rank me with whom you will;
put me to doing, put me to suffering;
let me be employed for you or laid aside for you,
exalted for you or brought low for you;
let me be full, let me be empty,
let me have all these things, let me have nothing;
I freely and wholeheartedly yield all things to your pleasure
   and disposal.

And now, glorious and blessed God, Father, Son and Holy
   Spirit,
you are mine and I am yours.
So be it.
And the covenant which I have made on earth,
let it be ratified in heaven.
Amen.[11]

Leader

Lewis summed it up dramatically:

> 'Die before you die. There is no chance after.'[12]

During the following music, you may like to take a seed and
plant it in the soil as a symbol of your willingness to continue
in your journey of following Christ.

Music or Song 4 or Silence

Leader

'Look for Christ and you will find him and with him everything else thrown in', or as Jesus said, 'I came that they might
have life, and have it abundantly.'[13]

   We were designed, through this pattern of death and rebirth,
to grow and flourish. With God there is always more.

Reader 2

When the children return to Narnia to rescue Prince Caspian
and they eventually meet Aslan again, they notice a change:

> 'Aslan,' said Lucy, 'you're bigger.'
>   'That is because you are older, little one,' he answered.
>   'Not because you are?'
>   'I am not. But every year you grow, you will find me
> bigger.'[14]

Reader 3

In the final Narnia story after the Last Battle the children arrive
in Aslan's country and find it like the old Narnia they knew, but

brighter, clearer, deeper and much much larger.

> 'I see,' [Lucy] said at last thoughtfully, 'I see now. This garden is like the Stable. It is far bigger inside than it was outside.'
>
> 'Of course …,' said the Faun. 'The farther up and the farther in you go, the bigger everything gets. The inside is larger than the outside.'[15]

Leader

Look at the bare winter branches – empty, pruned, apparently barren – and remember that they are still able to bear rich fruit.*

Music or Song 5 or Silence

Leader

Leave now to continue your journey,
knowing that you cannot know where it will take you.
Leave now in hope,
knowing that out of the deadness of winter, rich fruit can still come.
Leave now in gratitude,
knowing that you can trust in a pattern laid down before the beginning of time.
Leave now in fellowship,
taking with you in your heart these others with whom you have shared through Lent.
Journey together or alone, through joy and pain, absence and presence, death and rebirth.
Rejoice as you travel, for what awaits you is far bigger than you can possibly imagine.
Go now in peace, to love and serve the Lord.

All

In the name of Christ,
Amen.

Optional Extra

Living in a sceptical age
(Prince Caspian)

To start you thinking

Facing the disbelief of others

> Trust in the Lord with all your heart. Never rely on what
> you think you know. Remember the Lord in everything
> you do and he will show you the right way. Never let your-
> self think that you are wiser than you are; simply obey the
> Lord and refuse to do wrong. (Proverbs 3:5–7)[1]

Many hundreds of years have gone by. The castle of Cair
Paravel is in ruins and the Golden Age when the Sons of Adam
and the Daughters of Eve were Kings and Queens of Narnia is
just a faint memory. Stories of a White Witch who made the
land perpetual winter, and a lion named Aslan who defeated
her and brought the spring, are seen as fanciful legends.

This is the scenario at the opening of C. S. Lewis's second
chronicle of Narnia, *Prince Caspian*, and it has echoes of a
time very much like our own. The events of Jesus' earthly life
are two thousand years distant. Guidance by pillars of fire
and commandments on tablets of stone seem even more
anachronistic.

Incredible grand stories

The worldview of our age has been described as post-modernist – a view summed up as: 'incredulity toward meta-narratives',[2] or in other words, refusal to believe in anything resembling 'grand stories', coherent explanatory worldviews. Christianity is just such a worldview, and therefore not to be trusted.

The post-modern label was not around in C. S. Lewis's day, but the sceptical attitude certainly was. He even remarked that it was more to be found among theologians than in any other academic discipline![3]

And interestingly, it was indeed a theologian, Don Cupitt, who coined a defining phrase of post-modernism, that 'Capital T truth is dead'.[4]

Lewis had nothing against rationalism – his writings show the most rigorous application of reason and argument. Indeed, he was convinced that Christian faith was entirely rational and that it was scepticism itself that was irrational:

> I have no rational ground for going back on the arguments that convinced me of God's existence: but the irrational deadweight of my old sceptical habits, and the spirit of this age and the cares of the day, steal away all my lively feeling of the truth …[5]

Influential cynics

Even the most faithful and committed of believers are far more influenced by the spirit of the age than many would care to admit. Perhaps far more so now than in Lewis's day, as the media in its many forms bombards us so constantly and so subtly.

Not that scepticism of itself is necessarily wrong. When it leads to scientific questioning and refusal to accept assumptions or assertions with nothing to back them, it can only be a good thing. But when it becomes blanket cynicism, an allegation that nothing *can* be known, a refusal to contemplate anything outside of our own limited experience, then it becomes a crippling and destructive force.

Christianity and science are not, as a few atheists with loud voices would have us believe, at odds. Rather, as Lewis puts it:

> In science we have been reading only the notes to a poem; in Christianity we find the poem itself.[6]

Science tells us 'what' and 'how' in the material sense – and we need to know that. Christianity addresses the 'why', but also the 'what' and 'how' in a spiritual sense. How are we to live? What are the things that really matter?

In the story of *Prince Caspian*, Peter and Susan are moving into adolescence and Lucy's determination to trust in Aslan is beginning to seem a little childish. Especially when she claims she can see him and they most certainly can't. To Trumpkin the dwarf, talk of invisible magic lions is all 'bilge and bean-stalks'.[7] But when they eventually discover Aslan's path to be the right one, it is a different story.

Unlikely wisdom

Both the Old and New Testaments assert that God's wisdom can often be entirely different from our own. Indeed, as Lewis points out, the New Testament claims that:

> '... you should become fools so that you may become wise. For the wisdom of this world is foolishness with God.'[8]

But it also asserts that this topsy-turvy wisdom can be proven by its outcomes. Those who obey God flourish like trees planted at the waterside, says the Psalmist.[9] 'Wisdom is vindicated by all her children,' says Jesus,[10] or as others have paraphrased it, 'God's wisdom is proved right by its results.'

In order to find that out it is necessary to trust in the unlikely wisdom, to believe that the road less travelled[11] might just be the right one.

Group Session

Introduction   *1 min*
The story of *Prince Caspian* is set many hundreds of years
after the Golden Age when Aslan defeated the White Witch and
the four Pevensie children ruled as Kings and Queens of
Narnia. The land has fallen into disorder and been conquered
by the Telmarines, who have banished the talking beasts and
trees. Only a small remnant remain, hiding deep in the forests.
Most people think stories of Aslan and of the old times are just
myths and legends.

In some ways our age is very similar: two thousand long
years after Jesus walked the earth, post-modern scepticism has
become the dominant western worldview and Christians are
often seen as a beleaguered remnant. How is it possible to
exercise faith in an age such as this?

Brainstorm   *8 mins*
Many sceptical voices are raised against religion these days.
What are those voices that challenge your faith most? From
whom and from where do they come? List those that challenge
you most.

**Film clip 1: *Prince Caspian* – When others think you're
mad**   *2 mins*
Lucy thinks she sees Aslan, but the others don't believe her.

Discuss   *5 mins*
The film doesn't show us whether Lucy really did see Aslan. If
you had been one of the other children or Trumpkin the dwarf,
would you have believed her? What are your reasons?

Reflect and share   *10 mins*
God has given us minds that work in both rational and intuitive
ways. Think for a moment about which way is most dominant

in your own personality. How do you react to other people who think in different ways? Share as you feel able.

Discuss *10 mins*
Picture a scenario where you are working with others to reach a goal and one of the team is convinced God has shown a path you should follow. To you it seems a wacky idea. How would you evaluate whether their suggestion is right?

Reading: John 20:24–29 *1 min*

Discuss *10 mins*
Jesus said 'Blessed are those who have not seen and yet have believed.'

How often do you think we, as Christians, should expect to 'see' incontrovertible proof of God at work in our lives? Often, sometimes, hardly ever, never? Take a vote then discuss your reasons.

Film clip 2: *Prince Caspian* – When things don't happen as you expect *8 mins*
Lucy meets Aslan.

Brainstorm *5 mins*
In each of these two film clips one of the children asks Lucy why she thinks they didn't see Aslan. Her answers are 'Maybe you weren't looking' and 'Maybe you didn't really want to'.

Most of us have times in our lives when we could really do without a spiritual encounter. When and why might that be the case? List as many circumstances as you can.

Discuss *10 mins*
'Things never happen the same way twice,' says Aslan to Lucy.

How much should the way we practise and express our faith change to accommodate a changing world, and how much should it stick to tried-and-tested words and ways?

Reflect and share *10 mins*

'Every year you grow, so shall I,' says Aslan to Lucy.

In what way has your view of God changed over the years? Has it grown or diminished, broadened or narrowed?

Meditation *10 mins*

Reader 1

The apostle Paul says:

> So we are always confident; even though we know that while we are at home in the body we are away from the Lord – for we walk by faith, not by sight.[12]

Reader 2

C. S. Lewis suggests that often:

> the conflict is not between faith and reason but between faith and sight.[13]

We are told by someone trustworthy that the cliff path is safe, and our reason tells us to believe them. But it looks scary and so we waver. Lewis says:

> Faith … is the art of holding on to things your reason has once accepted, in spite of your changing moods.[14]

In the silence, ask God to help you to hold on to your faith despite sceptical looks or sarcastic comments, despite fluctuating moods or limited vision.

Silence *(1 min)*

Reader 3

In a book memorably entitled *Your God is too small*, the writer J. B. Phillips says:

> The trouble with many people today is that they have not found a God big enough for their needs. While their experience of life has grown in a score of directions, and

their mental horizons have been expanded to the point of
bewilderment by world events and by scientific discoveries, their ideas of God have remained largely static.[15]

God is not too small, but our ideas of him often are. We need
not be afraid to explore beyond the safe simplistic view of faith
we began with. Like Lucy with Aslan, every year that we grow,
we will discover God to be far bigger than we ever imagined.

Has your view of God got stuck?

Silence *(1 min)*

Leader

In order to live wisely and well, we could do no better than
follow the advice of the apostle Peter:

Grow in the grace and knowledge of our Lord and Saviour
Jesus Christ.[16]

Reader 4

Prayer

Lord, forgive us.
We are often scared that our faith will look foolish,
often uncertain how to marry our reason and our intuition,
often fearful that when faced by the big wide sceptical world
    our God may turn out to be too small.
Often clinging to familiar formulae, rather than learning
    that God rarely works in the same way twice.
Lord, help us
to be prepared to trust where we cannot see,
prepared to live by faith and not just the accepted logic,
prepared to discover you in places we had never expected,
prepared to be believing people in a sceptical age.
Help us to grow in grace and knowledge
in the name of Christ,
Amen.

Silence *(2 mins)*

To take it further

Dealing with our own uncertainties

> So we are always confident; even though we know that
> while we are at home in the body we are away from the
> Lord – for we walk by faith, not by sight.
>
> (2 Corinthians 5:7)

'Why didn't you show yourself?' asks Lucy of Aslan when she
finally gets to meet him face to face. 'Why didn't you come
roaring in and save us?'[17]

'Things never happen the same way twice,' is Aslan's
unapologetic answer.[18]

For many Christians their initial entry into faith is accom-
panied by some clear sign or remarkable personal experience
that tells them they have truly met with God. Unfortunately for
some, they spend the rest of their lives wishing they were back
there, or trying to recapture that first dramatic encounter.

Aslan does not come roaring straight in to save the Narnians
because his purpose this time is different. For Prince Caspian
it is preparation for becoming King, for Peter a crash course in
leadership, for others it is a learning experience in how to work
as a team with creatures quite unlike themselves.

Developing through our mistakes

And God does not continue to give us dramatic spiritual experiences and incontrovertible guidance for the same reason.
He wants us to learn and become strong, to develop our character toward the good, to be humble toward others and to tune
our antennae toward the Holy Spirit. And happily or not for us,
he is more than willing for us to learn by our mistakes!

The apostle Paul understood that if we are 'at home in the
body' we must, by definition, be 'away from the Lord'. For us
to become fully earthed human beings, God must keep his

distance, because as C.S. Lewis explained:

> God's presence in any but the faintest and most mitigated
> degree would override our will and defeat his purpose.[19]

If we really lived all the time directly in God's presence, we would be so overwhelmed by the immensity of God's wisdom that we would never develop our own. Moreover, it would be so wonderful that we would probably become intensely soppy and irritating to anyone who came near us!

Confident despite the unknown

And so our life of faith has to be lived by hints and rumours from another dimension, wisdom from an ancient book, advice from others on the journey alongside us, and just now and then, often when we least expect it and in the most unlikely way, an unmistakeable encounter with our Lord. But it is enough. All these combine to tell us that we can be confident.

There will be times when we will need to cling to that confidence. We will need to have learned the art of hanging on to words of God that have already proved themselves to us.

Because sometimes God's operations in our lives may appear anything but wise and far from beneficial. Despite these difficulties, says Lewis:

> If human life is in fact ordered by a beneficent being
> whose knowledge of our real needs and of the way in
> which they can be satisfied infinitely exceeds our own …
> it will be our highest prudence to give him our confi-
> dence.[20]

To be human is to live without seeing the full picture.

Scepticism means trusting nothing. Faith means trusting in someone.

Leader's Notes

Introduction

The way the groups work

The timings for each session add up to a total of around 1 hour 30 minutes, but you will have to keep very strictly to time and not allow anyone to wander off the point, if you want to achieve this. The sessions will work more comfortably if a total of 2 hours is allowed.

Each group session has three basic types of questions:

Brainstorm
Try and get as many quick-fire answers (just one word or phrase) as possible. It will help to have a large pad of drawing paper (A2 size is fine for a smallish group) and appoint some-one as scribe to write down the answers. Don't get into too much discussion on these questions.

Discuss
This is the point at which ideas and opinions can be batted back and forth.

Reflect and share
These questions are intended to bring out experiences rather than opinions. Allow 30 seconds–1 minute of silence first before inviting people to share their experience. Try and resist too much discussion, and certainly avoid giving advice, although if one person's sharing of their experience prompts someone else to share, that's fine in moderation.

Meditation

Each session ends with a time of quiet and meditation for about 5–10 minutes. You may like to look out some suitable recorded music to play, if you feel that your group is uncomfortable with silence. (Even if they're not, a few moments of quiet music at the end of a busy day is incredibly therapeutic!)

The problems of technology

DVDs may be an advance in technology over videotape in some ways, but unfortunately not when it comes to playing selected clips. Each of the group sessions is based on the need to play two clips, one from each movie, and to do that smoothly with DVDs will require a certain amount of forethought and possibly even practice.

Make sure you familiarise yourself with the DVD player and TV you are to use before the session begins and people start to arrive. This is especially important if your group is not always in the same place, and you will be using different machines!

The best idea is always to have the first clip set up ready and waiting in pause mode before the session begins.

The best time to change over to the second clip is during the first 'reflect and share' session. Ask people to close their eyes as they reflect, so that you can change DVDs without distracting them. (NB: Ensure you have muted the TV sound before you do this!)

Most clips start at the beginning of a DVD 'chapter', but some do not and this becomes more difficult. In this event, spool through from the beginning of the chapter beforehand to the place you want and leave the machine set on pause. (In one case, it will be easier to spool back from the following chapter.)

If you are also planning to play a track from a CD for the meditation, don't forget to ensure that this is set up ready before the session starts as well.

The gift of listening

The greatest gift you may be able to give anyone else in the context of this group is the gift of being listened to – and being heard.

If you are unsure of what someone is trying to say, reflect back what you thought you heard, preferably using different words without changing the meaning. If in doubt, ask a question to try and tease out the background behind a particular comment.

Notice the attitudes and feelings involved as well as a person's words. Be aware of body language and what it is saying. Listen carefully for what is *not* being said.

Resist the urge to respond with your own message, opinion or advice. You are there to facilitate others and chances are that someone else in the group has something just as valuable to offer.

If you sense that there is some deeper issue behind someone's words then try and find out afterwards if it is something that requires further prayer or counselling. You need not be the one providing further help, but make it your business to seek it out for them if they wish it.

If you find that the group are particularly bad at listening to each other, then in desperation, here are a couple of techniques:

- have a small item – a shell, a pebble, a toy mouse – and make a rule that only the person holding it can speak;
- find some noise-making implement – a bell, a whistle, a hooter – and agree a maximum length for each contribution. Then appoint someone as time-keeper and noise-maker when the speaker's time is up.

The acceptance of difference

Particularly for this course, which looks at some issues where doctrinal differences are acute, it's important to recognise that people may be coming from very varied backgrounds in terms of their Christian experience and beliefs.

In an ecumenical group this is especially important, as it may include everything from wishy-washy liberals to happy-clappy fundamentalists. (OK, those last two descriptions were appalling stereotypes – but I included them on purpose, to remind you that we do all arrive with preconceptions and prejudices about people different from ourselves.) What these sessions, and especially you as a leader, are aiming to do is to break down these differences and concentrate on what we have in common, our humanity and our relationship with a God who is far above such narrowmindedness.

Bear in mind, too, that in these days of church as a consumer product, even within one congregation, people will probably have arrived there by very different routes and via very different experiences of Christianity.

If necessary, when differences become apparent, try and tease out what experiences lie behind people's beliefs and opinions.

The agreement of ground rules

Some suggested ground rules are given in the Introduction on p. 11. At the first session, it may be a good idea to go over these and see if people agree to them or want to add or alter them in any way. Once agreed, remind the group of them when necessary and ensure they are adhered to.

Week One:
Living in the shadows

Introducing the course
Check whether everyone has had a chance to see both movies right through. If not, is there a chance for them to borrow them between sessions?

Explain the different types of questions as outlined on p. 93.

Take some time to discuss and agree the ground rules for the group as outlined on p. 11.

Reinforce the idea that participants should try and make time to read the 'before' and 'after' chapters each week.

Getting to know one another

This can only be a brief exercise, but exactly how long you devote to it will obviously vary depending on how much the group members know each other, if at all.

Go round the room and let people simply introduce themselves (and what church they are from, if appropriate) and their expectations from the course, e.g.:

> My name is ... (and I'm from ...) and how I would most like to grow in my spiritual life this Lent is ...

Feedback from readings

Ask if anyone has any feedback, questions or issues for discussion from what they have read of the course so far. Don't discuss it now, but make a note for later during the session.

Film clip 1: *Narnia* – Living in a cold world

In: Chapter 4 beginning – going towards Mr Tumnus' home.
Out: '... warmer now than I've felt in 100 years. Now go.' Lucy goes from lamp-post to wardrobe.

Lucy has gone through the wardrobe for the first time and met Mr Tumnus the faun, who takes her to his home for tea and sardines. He explains that in Narnia it is 'always winter but never Christmas'. He tells her of the good old days and plays his pan pipes. The music and the images of dancing figures in the flames bewitch her and she falls asleep. She wakes to find the fire gone and Mr Tumnus sobbing, and explaining that he was planning to kidnap her. However, he takes her back to the lamp-post, telling her that the White Witch might even now know about her. 'Even some of the trees are on her side.' He says he is glad to have met her. 'You've made me feel warmer than I've felt in 100 years.'

Discuss
In what ways might lack of a belief in a personal devil damage or strengthen the way we live our Christian life?
The obvious question behind this is whether the individual members of the group actually believe in a personal devil or not. It might be good to allow some time to find this out before proceeding with the actual question posed. Any discussion of the Devil might easily stray into a discussion of the occult or witchcraft. If this happens, try and bring the discussion back to subtle everyday temptations rather than dramatic supernatural happenings.

Belief in a personal devil might damage the way we live out our Christian life by:

- allowing people to blame their failings on an outside influence and thereby excuse themselves.
- seeming so irrational and archaic as to compromise intelligence.

Belief in a personal devil might strengthen Christian living by:

- making people realise that there is a much bigger spiritual battle going on, of which they are part.
- making people realise that they are always being tempted in subtle ways and therefore need to take special care to pray for God's help and guidance.
- making people unite against a common enemy, rather than automatically blaming and mistrusting each other.
- making people believe that evil is an outside force to be resisted rather than just 'human nature'.

Discuss
How does Lucy show humanity to Mr Tumnus?

- by trusting him
- by being interested in his home, his father etc.

• by lending him her handkerchief.

Reflect and share

Think of one small touch of warmth and humanity from another, recently or in the past, that has made a difference to your life.

Allow 1 minute for reflection. Suggest that people close their eyes as they reflect. This then gives you as leader the opportunity to set up the next video clip, selecting the right scene and leaving it on pause. (Don't forget to mute the TV sound first!)

Film clip 2: *Shadowlands* – Living in the 'shadowlands'

In: Chapter 2 beginning – Lewis and Warnie in café.
Out: '… I almost don't know what to say to you.' Warnie: 'Good Lord.'

Lewis and his brother Warnie meet Joy Gresham for the first time in a café. They are nervous about having their safe bachelor world interrupted. Joy begins to challenge Lewis who says he enjoys a good fight. 'Yes, but how long since you lost?' Later they take her on a tour of the colleges. She tells him how impassioned she was with the cause of the Spanish civil war: 'Wasn't everyone?' Lewis says he 'must have been otherwise engaged at the time'. He tells her about the custom of May Day singing, acknowledging that he has never actually seen it. Joy asks, 'Do you go round with your eyes shut?'

Brainstorm

In what ways does this film clip imply that Lewis might be insulated from real experience and not living life to the full?

• He is easily embarrassed by meeting with a woman/American.
• He doesn't want Joy to disrupt his routine existence.
• He might not be comfortable with debates that he cannot win.
• The passionate Communist/Fascist debate of the Spanish

Civil War seems to have passed him by.
• He has never bothered to see the May morning ritual, despite living in Oxford for many years.

This view is encapsulated in the comment Joy makes, 'Do you go around with your eyes shut?' However, it is worth pointing out that this clip also paints a picture of Lewis as gentlemanly and courteous and willing to admit his faults.

It is important to reinforce that this is only a simplified film version of Lewis – the real person was undoubtedly somewhat different. His writings bear out that, like most of us, in some ways he may have been reserved and stuck in a rut while in others he was passionate and adventurous.

Discuss
What difference, if any, might a belief in a future life make to our understanding of life to the full now?
It might be useful to begin by establishing how people view the idea of a future life. For instance: do they have a strong belief, no belief, or never think about it?

Differences brought about by a belief in a future life could be:

• the idea that we have an eternity to experience an even fuller life frees us from the selfish need to experience as much as we can now.
• conversely, fear of judgement could make us live timidly and narrowly.

Week Two:
Living with the beyond

NB: You will need to run through the first film clip to find the exact place, so be sure to do this before people arrive. Leave the DVD player on pause. You can turn the TV itself off.

Introduction

Review ground rules. Ask if people have any issues arising that they would like to comment on or discuss. Decide whether they can be quickly looked at right away, whether they will fit in any specific part of the forthcoming discussion, or leave to the end just before the meditation.

Film clip 1: *Shadowlands* – Living with the unattainable
In: Chapter 1 – after credits – long shot of Oxford at dawn, then exterior of college building.
Out: after '… got to catch my train.'

Lewis is giving a tutorial about the medieval tale of a lover's search for a perfect rosebud hidden in a walled garden. He contends that it is all about 'unattainability'. 'The most intense joy lies not in the having but in the desiring. The delight that never fades, the bliss that is most eternal, is only yours when what you desire is most out of reach.'

We next see Lewis in a pub with his academic colleagues who are mildly teasing him about his Narnia tales. The clergyman present comments that the imagery is Christian, but Lewis corrects him, 'No, Harry. It is what it is. It's just magical.' Lewis begins to describe going through the wardrobe into the snowy world of Narnia: 'a gateway to a magical world'.

Reflect and share
Have you had any experiences, 'magical' or otherwise?
NB: Suggest that people close their eyes to think about this. While they are doing this set up the next clip, remembering to mute the TV sound first!

Remind people if necessary that this is a time to share without feedback, comment or advice. Allow them freedom to share their experiences however off-the-wall or inarticulate. However, if anyone should happen to stray into anything veering on occult or spiritualism, it is probably best to head the discussion off in another direction and pick it up later with the individual concerned.

Discuss

> 'The most intense joy lies not in the having but in the desiring.'

It may be worth referring to Augustine's statement (quoted later in the meditation) that 'You have made us for yourself, and our heart is restless until it finds its rest in you.'

Another interesting point that may be worth bringing up, if no one else does, is that our entire consumerist society only works on the premise that people are never satisfied – that as soon as they have what they desire, they begin to desire something else.

Discuss

Do you find it hard to think in terms of 'storing up treasure in heaven'?

It may be necessary to backtrack on this question and begin by asking what Jesus meant by the statement. Are we talking about spiritual 'Brownie points' or something a little deeper and more complex? It may have more to do with our value system and living by God's values and not worldly ones.

Film clip 2: *Narnia* – Living with the unbelievable

In: Chapter 7, beginning, 'Peter, wake up.'
Out: after 'You're a family, aren't you? You might just start acting like one.'

Lucy has returned to the wardrobe, followed by Edmund who has met the White Witch. On their return, Lucy is relieved she now has someone else to back up her story, but Edmund denies having been to Narnia: 'You know what little children are like these days. They don't know when to stop pretending.' Peter tells the Professor of Lucy's story: 'Logically it's impossible.' 'What do they teach them these days?' mutters the Professor, suggesting that 'If she's not mad and she's not lying, then logically you should believe her.'

Discuss

Why do you think Edmund denied his experience of Narnia?

You may want to skip this question as it doesn't have a great deal to add to the theme. Alternatively, it may be useful to get people talking on an easier topic for a while.

Possible answers:

- he didn't want to give away what he had been doing – meeting the White Witch.
- he was too proud to admit an experience he had scorned previously.
- he wanted to look good in Peter's eyes.
- he wanted to get at Lucy.

Reflect and share

What makes you most convinced of a spiritual dimension to life?

Ideally, see if you can get a quick soundbite answer from everyone in the group on this one.

Discuss

What do you think are the things most responsible for people leaving the Christian faith?

This question could be something of a red herring, as obviously very often we can only guess at the answer. If you decide to take it up, don't get too bogged down in the wrongs of the Church. The interesting question is whether others or ourselves really make an effort to understand the Christian faith and reconcile it with reason, or just depend on vague feelings.

Week Three:
Living with the unexplained

NB: Because the first clip comes a fair way through the DVD chapter, ensure you have it set up and ready on pause, before the group starts – or preferably even before they arrive.

Film clip 1: *Shadowlands* – The purpose of suffering
In: Chapter 1 a fair way through, after scene in pub, at beginning of Lewis addressing meeting, before 'Yesterday I had a letter …'
Out: after '… the blows of the chisel make us perfect. Thank you.'

Lewis gives a lecture to a hall full of women, referring to an incident where a bus had ploughed into a column of young Royal Marine cadets. He quotes a correspondent: 'Where was God? Why didn't he stop it? Isn't he supposed to love us? Does God want us to suffer?' Lewis surmises, 'What if the answer is yes? I'm not sure that God particularly wants us to be happy. I think he wants us to love and to be loved. I think he wants us to grow up. I suggest that it is because God loves us that he gives us the gift of suffering … Pain is God's megaphone to rouse a deaf world. We are like blocks of stone out of which the sculptor carves perfect forms of men. The blows of his chisel which hurt us so much are what make us perfect.'

Reflect and share

> All the great religions were first preached and long practised in a world without chloroform.

You may need to remind the group that chloroform was one of the first and most primitive anaesthetics and that we now live in a world where anaesthetics, sophisticated painkillers and antibiotics have eliminated even more pain and suffering than Lewis envisaged. You don't need to reflect for 5 minutes as Lewis suggests; 2 minutes will probably do.

NB: In this or the other 'reflect and share', get people to close their eyes, and during this time set up the next film clip. Don't forget to mute the sound!

Discuss

> 'He was born blind so that God's power might be seen at work.'

Obviously we can only guess what Jesus might have meant or what the blind man's circumstances might have been. The group may need encouragement to use their imagination to picture different possibilities, and a reminder that this is a valid and often effective way of illuminating the story.

Film clip 2: *Narnia* – The purpose of sacrifice

In: beginning of Chapter 17 – Susan and Lucy see Aslan ascending to the stone table.

Out: after 'The great cat is dead!'

The White Witch has confronted Aslan and told him that ,according to their laws, the traitor, Edmund, must die. But after the Witch and Aslan have talked in private, Aslan emerges to say that 'she has renounced her claim on the son of Adam'. That night Lucy and Susan wake to see Aslan padding off. They follow and watch as Aslan approaches the stone table and evil mutant creatures shave him, bind him and haul him on to the stone table. The Witch scorns his apparent weakness: 'Did you honestly think you could save the human traitor? … Tomorrow we will take Narnia for ever. In that knowledge despair and die.' The knife plunges in and Aslan is killed.

Brainstorm

What similarities did you notice between this episode of Aslan's death and the story of the death of Jesus in the gospels?

To some more experienced Christians this might seem one of those questions where the answers are obvious. But encourage them to list similarities as quickly as they can. They will probably come up with more than they thought, and probably there are some people in the group for whom it is not so obvious at all.

Meditation music
There are so many possibilities here that it isn't worth making any particular suggestions, but gentle instrumental music is probably the best option.

Week Four:
Living with what we've been given

NB: Because you need to find the first film clip, it is important to set it up beforehand, i.e. before the meeting even starts. When you have found the right place then leave it set ready on pause.

Introduction
If getting through all the material is a problem, it might be worth reinforcing the ground rules of listening, rather than speaking too much.

Film clip 1: *Narnia* – The gift of a purpose
In: Chapter 11 some way in – children running from sled.
Out: Father Christmas leaves.

As the ice begins to thaw, the children meet with Father Christmas, who tells them that hope is weakening the Witch's power. He gives them gifts – for Lucy a phial of healing medicine and a dagger for protection; for Susan a bow and arrow,

'Trust and it will not easily miss', and a horn to call for help; for Peter a sword and a shield. 'They are tools, not toys, bear them well and wisely. Long live Aslan and merry Christmas.'

Discuss

'They are tools, not toys.'

Do today's children get too many toys or too much amusement? Do you think there is something wrong with our attitudes to childhood? If so, what?
Be careful to ensure that this doesn't come across as a criticism from the older generation to any parents of young children present.

Reflect and share

Have you ever been given a really good gift (material or spiritual) – one which has gone on enhancing your life rather than just giving temporary pleasure? What was special about it?
During this section get people to close their eyes to reflect and set up the next film clip in readiness. Again, leave it on pause.
NB: Because this clip is a bit difficult to find quickly, it might well be worth practising finding it before the meeting starts.

Film clip 2: *Shadowlands* – the gift of the present moment
In: Chapter 9 near end (go to chapter 10 and rewind). Car going to golden valley.
Out: Joy: '… that's the deal.' They kiss.

Lewis and Joy have gone to the Golden Valley at a time of Joy's remission from illness. Rain starts and they shelter in a barn. Lewis comments that he is 'not looking for anything else to happen, not wanting to be anywhere else. Here, now, that's enough.' Joy asks, 'That's your kind of happiness, isn't it?' and Lewis agrees that it is. She warns him, 'It isn't going to last, Jack.' He protests that they shouldn't think about it now and spoil the time they have. She claims that 'It doesn't spoil it. It makes it real ... What I'm trying to say is that the pain then is part of the happiness now. That's the deal.'

Reflect and share

Have you ever had an experience where pain and happiness (or joy) have gone hand in hand? Share it if you feel able.

I originally used only the word 'happiness', but felt that 'joy', an emotion with something of an ache and longing in it, as defined by Lewis (see Week 2: To start you thinking: Living with the beyond) was nearer the mark than plain happiness. Perhaps it would help to unpack both of these words a little.

Discuss

Is this sense of contentment the same as that expressed by Lewis in the film? If not, what is different?

The word 'contentment' has at least two different shades of meaning:

- a feeling of deep satisfaction.
- a willingness to accept what comes.

Probably Lewis means the former and Paul means the latter. Explore both or either as appropriate.

Week Five:
Living with absence

NB: Because the first film clip starts quite a way through a chapter, it is important to have it set up ready before the session starts. Find the right place and leave it on pause.

This session is quite strong stuff, especially for any who might recently have gone through bereavement or still have raw feelings about a time of grief. If you don't know already, perhaps it is worth finding out at the beginning of the session whether anyone is in that place right now. It is probably also worth reminding people to share with respect and sensitivity because these are such difficult issues.

Film clip 1: *Shadowlands* – **When belief is tested**
In: Chapter 10 funeral car going to cremation, quite a long way in.
Out: Lewis and Douglas hugging in attic, back view.

After Joy's death, Lewis meets a clergyman friend who says, 'I thank God for your faith, Jack. Only faith makes sense at a time like this.' Lewis says nothing. Later with Warnie he expresses his feelings that sufferings have no purpose after all. Warnie doesn't know what to say and Lewis responds 'Nothing, nothing to say. I know that now … Experience is a brutal teacher, but you learn, my God, you learn.' Later when academics are gathering in the common room, the clergyman again utters a platitude: 'Only God knows why these things happen.' Lewis explodes: 'God knows, but does God care?… We're rats in the cosmic laboratory. I've no doubt that the experiment is for our own good, but it still makes God the vivisectionist, doesn't it?… It won't do! It's a bloody awful mess and that's all there is to it.' Later walking home, Warnie tells Lewis that he needs to talk to Douglas, Joy's son. Lewis finds Douglas sitting in front of the wardrobe that he now believes holds no magic. Together they hug and cry.

Brainstorm
In what ways do people express concern and consolation?
Responses in the film clip are:
Clergyman: 'Thank God for your faith. Only faith makes sense … I know.'
Warnie: 'I don't know what to say.'
Academic: 'Better sooner than later.'
Academic: 'All for the best.'
Christopher: 'I'm sorry.'
Master: 'We're all deeply sorry.'

Clergyman: 'Life must go on.'

Christopher: 'Anything I can do?'

Clergyman: 'Only God knows why these things happen.'

Warnie: 'Talk to him' (reminding the grieving person to look beyond their own pain).

Lewis: 'It doesn't seem fair' (to Douglas).

Lewis: 'That's OK' (allowing Douglas disbelief).

Lewis: 'You can't hold on to things, you have to let them go.'

A hug and crying together.

Reflect and share

Which of the responses listed above were the most helpful?

Try to extract the understanding that different people express grief in different ways. Also, even within one individual's reaction to loss, grief comes in waves, so that what is appropriate one moment may be inappropriate the next. The key is perhaps to show care in whatever way, as long as it is genuine care. The major thing to avoid is an assumption that you *know* how the person is feeling. You may be able to guess, but you may be wrong. Sharing from your own experience can be helpful, but only if you are carefully listening as well – *not* if you are offering it as a prescription for someone else.

Reflect and share

Have there been times in your life when the sheer hurt of something blocked out any sense of God?

Ask people to close their eyes during this reflection and during this time set up the next film clip.

Discuss

How do you react to the knowledge that Jesus faced a sense of being abandoned?

One of our test group members came up with the interesting perception that perhaps that moment of abandonment was when Jesus was the most fully human of all.

Film clip 2: *Narnia* – When God is absent
In: Chapter 23 beginning – mermaids, Cair Paravel.
Out: Sunset.

After the grand ceremony where the children have been
crowned kings and queens of Narnia, Lucy and Mr Tumnus are
out on the balcony of Cair Paravel when they see Aslan at
twilight going off over the sand. Mr Tumnus says, 'Don't
worry, we'll see him again.' 'When?' asks Lucy. 'In time,'
answers Mr Tumnus. 'One time he'll be here and the next he
won't. After all, he's not a tame lion – but he is good.'

Brainstorm
Why might God's 'absence' be good for us?
Perhaps 'apparent absence' or 'lack of communication' might
be a better description of what is happening at these times, but
try and let group members tease that out for themselves.

Discuss (Optional)
Do you think the Church has tried to 'tame' God?
Take care with this question as it is likely to go off at something
of a tangent from the main themes of the session and could lead
to a 'being critical of church' session. If you do tackle it, take
it back to the individual's own reactions and the tendency in
all of us to want to pin down God and make him more predictable and available to us. Go back to Lewis's depiction of
Aslan and remind that God is much greater than any of us can
imagine.

Reflect and share (Optional)
*Does the idea of a sudden unexpected meeting with Jesus
frighten or excite you?*
Perhaps the reflecting is the most important part here, rather
than the sharing. Again, if you do tackle it, beware of it taking
people off at a tangent.

Holy Week:
Meditative Service

Timing

The actual written material of this service takes about 20 minutes to read through. That means that by the time you have added in recorded music or silence or songs, you have something around the length of 30–45 minutes. Obviously you could usefully add more silent pauses at other times if you wish to extend it to an hour. You might like to consider replaying film clip 2 from *The Lion the Witch and the Wardrobe* used in Week Three, showing the death and return to life of Aslan. Alternatively, you could read some of the account from Chapter 15 of the book. If so, the best point within the service would be after the verses from John 12 that end 'I if lifted up from the earth, will draw all people to myself'.

Symbols

Arrange a table in the centre or at the front with the following symbols:

- seeds
- tray or pot of soil
- some branches that look dead but have the very faintest signs of coming into life
- a crucifix.

Try and find branches from some sort of fruit-bearing tree or shrub: apple, pear, vine, cherry, raspberry canes etc.

Have available but hidden a bowl of the appropriate fruit. Bring it out and place on the table at the point marked * before the final music/song/silence. At the end of the service, invite people to eat the fruit. (You might even like to have a few chocolate eggs also available for eating, hidden under the fruit!)

Ideally it would be great if the pot of planted seeds could then be kept so that people might be able to see them growing as the months go on. In this case, you need to make sure they are seeds that are easy to grow, that the pot is suitable for their long-term growth and that someone will continue to take responsibility for watering them. If people are to put the seeds into the soil with their hands, then a cloth for hand-wiping would be helpful. Otherwise you might like to provide a trowel.

Recorded music or songs

You could use all recorded music or all songs or a mix of both. You could replace both of them with silence throughout or in one or two slots.

I don't claim to be much of a music expert, and anyway, you will probably have ideas of your own, but following are a few suggestions.

For recorded music, I would suggest Carl Jenkins' *Requiem* as a possibility. This is quite strong and unusual music which is less likely to fade into the background. It may be distracting, though, if you have a group who are familiar with the meaning of the Latin words.

Another possibility is Margaret Rizza's *Icons 1*. This is an instrumental album specifically designed as a background for worship or reflection (and would also be ideal for the music slots in earlier group sessions).

I have put suggested tracks from these albums for each slot. Use about 2–3 minutes worth for each slot and be sure to fade out *very gently* when the time is up. Nothing is worse than an abrupt jolt out of meditative music.

As for singing, obviously that will depend on what people

know and whether they like modern or traditional, but I have at least tried to suggest a mix.

Slot 1: The pattern of death and rebirth
Music
Jenkins: Track 1 – Introit
Rizza: Track 7 – 'O Lord, Listen to my prayer'

Song
'Now the green blade riseth', 115 in *New English Hymnal*. This may not be one that is sung regularly, but the old folk tune is probably familiar and the words are ideal.

Slot 2: Crucifixion
Music
Jenkins: Track 7 – Lacrimosa
Rizza: Track 9 – Kyrie eleison

Song
'O sacred head sore wounded'

Slot 3: Resurrection
Music
Jenkins: Track 5 – Confutatis. (Track is slightly less than 3 minutes, so could be played to the end.)
Rizza: Track 2 – Magnificat

Song
'Led like a lamb to the slaughter', Graham Kendrick

Slot 4: Recommitment
Music
Jenkins: Track 9 – Pie Jesu
Rizza: Track 5 – O give thanks

Song
'The Servant King', Graham Kendrick

Slot 5: Future promise
Music
Jenkins: Track 13 – In Paradisum
Rizza: Track 10 – A blessing

Song
'Amazing Grace'

Optional Extra:
Living in a sceptical age
(Prince Caspian)

This session focuses around issues brought up in the film *The Chronicles of Narnia: Prince Caspian.* It is not essential for the whole group to have seen the whole film beforehand, but obviously it is preferable, so if you plan to do this session, try and either lend the DVD out to participants before the meeting or schedule in a group viewing. It *is* essential that you as leader have seen it. Be aware that this film differs from the book rather more than its predecessor did. I have tried to focus discussion around parts that the book and the film do have in common.

Unfortunately the DVD was not released at the time of this edition going to press, so exact timings for the clips cannot be given. Look on DLT website for timing information, etc.

Brainstorm
What are the voices that challenge your faith most?
People may think of specific names, for example, writers such as Richard Dawkins or Philip Pullman, or specific programmes in the media, social commentators, even liberal theologians. It may be personal comments from teachers, work colleagues,

family or friends. It may be participants' own inner voice and their own personal scepticism that challenge most.

Film clip 1

In: (fairly early in the film) After the four children and Trumpkin the dwarf arrive at a steep and impassable ravine and before they begin to argue about what to do.

Out: After the others begin to follow Peter walking away and Lucy looks back but sees nothing there.

Peter, Susan, Edmund and Lucy have met Trumpkin the dwarf and together are journeying to find Prince Caspian. The river that was easy to cross back in their previous Narnian experience is now impassable. While they are arguing about what to do, Lucy looks up and exclaims that she can see Aslan across the ravine. The others can see nothing (and we don't see what she sees either) When she looks again she can see nothing either. But she insists that he was there and is sure that he wanted them to follow him. This appears impossible and the others are not convinced. Peter exercises gentle but decisive leadership and heads them off in the other more logical direction.

Reflect and Share

Rational or intuitive – how do you react to people who think in different ways to you?

Anyone who has taken part in a Myers-Briggs personality indicator type test may have some background knowledge on this. To summarise somewhat simplistically, this is based on Jung's theory that information gathering is done in two different ways: 'Sensing', which means gathering information based on what we can see and hear; as opposed to 'Intuition', gathering more abstract impressions and relying on flashes of insight. Jung also divides decision-making functions into similar alternatives: 'Thinking', which tends to look at options in a detached and objective way; as opposed to 'Feeling', which tends towards decisions based on empathy and a desire for harmony.

Discuss

How do you react to a team member who believes God has shown them what to you seems a wacky way forward?

Some means of evaluating might be: looking at the 'track-record' of the person in question, asking if anyone else has the same sense of direction, seeing whether scripture has anything to say, taking a vote, praying, asking for advice from others.

Discuss

How often should we expect to see proof of God?

Be sensitive here about people coming from different sorts of church background, also those who are new in their faith, compared to those further along the road, or those who have had some sort of disappointment or setback to their faith.

Note that the word 'should' is ambiguous. It could mean claims made in the Bible, the demands others put on us, or our own expectations. This might need teasing out.

Film clip 2

In: (Sometime after the previous clip) The children and Trumpkin lay down to sleep around a fire. Come in just before Susan says: 'Why do you think I didn't see Aslan?'

Out: Just after Lucy is grabbed from behind by Peter.

The party has followed the logical route downriver to where they expect to find a ford. They discover the Telmarine army there, building a bridge, and have to withdraw rapidly. They retrace their steps to the place of Lucy's sighting of Aslan and discover a path down and up the other side of the ravine. Having crossed, they lay down round a bonfire.

In response to Susan's question, Lucy queries whether she really wanted to see Aslan. Susan admits some ambivalence about being back in Narnia, doubting whether it will last.

Some time later as night moves through to dawn, Lucy wakes and follows the blossom she sees swirling from the trees to a meeting with Aslan. He tells her that he will grow as she does and that things never happen the same way twice.

The film cuts to Lucy waking again by the fire. Maybe it was only a dream. She rises again, quietly calling for Aslan. Peter pulls her down because he thinks he sees an enemy. In fact, it is Prince Caspian.

Brainstorm

When and why could we really do without a spiritual encounter?

Few Christians admit to shunning an encounter with God, yet most of us employ avoidance techniques at one time or another. Reasons expressed may be: feeling guilty, being busy or pre-occupied, tiredness, not wanting to face a challenge.

Discuss

How much should the way we practise or express our faith change to accommodate a changing world?

'The way we practise or express our faith' is deliberately vague. It could lead to many issues: modes of worship, archaic language, fundamentalist doctrine, women priests or homo-sexuality.

It may be good to refer back to the introductory chapter to this section where it talks about a post-modernist worldview and changing views of truth. Other factors to consider might be: living in a multi-faith culture; lack of education about the Bible or Christianity in schools, reduced attention spans in a television age, discomfort with jargon etc. There may be other practical considerations, such as difficulties of getting to church when both partners in a family are working all week.

References

Extracts by C. S. Lewis copyright © C. S. Lewis Pte. Ltd. Reprinted by permission.

Introduction: Preparing for an uncomfortable Lent
1. *The Lion, the Witch and the Wardrobe*, ch 17, para 20.
2. *Mere Christianity*, book 1, ch 5, para 4.
3. ibid.

Background: Discovering the man and his world
1. *The Screwtape Letters*, ch 21, para 4.
2. *Surprised by Joy*, ch 1, para 6.
3. *Mere Christianity*, book 3, ch 3, para 4.
4. *A Grief Observed*, ch 3, para 29.
5. *Mere Christianity*, book 2, ch 3, para 2.
6. *Surprised by Joy*, ch 1, para 8.
7. William Kirkpatrick, quoted in *C. S. Lewis: the Authorised and Revised Biography* by Roger Lancelyn Green and Walter Hooper.
8. *The Last Battle*, ch 16, para 52.
9. *Surprised by Joy*, ch 2, para 16.
10. ibid., ch 14, para 123.
11. ibid., ch 15, para 6.
12. ibid., ch 15, para 8.
13. *Mere Christianity*, book 3, ch 5, para 7.
14. ibid., book 3, ch 6, para 10.
15. ibid., book 1, ch 5, para 2.
16. *The Problem of Pain*, ch 1, para 15.
17. *Mere Christianity*, book 2, ch 4, para 7.
18. ibid., book 4, ch 11, para 15.

Week One: Living in the shadows
1. *The Screwtape Letters*, ch 7, para 2.

2. ibid., Preface, para 2.
3. *Book of Common Prayer*, 'Collect for the 4th Sunday after Trinity'.
4. *The Screwtape Letters*, ch 12, para 5.
5. ibid., ch 12, para 6.
6. *The Last Battle*, ch 15, para 36 & ch 16 para 52.
7. *The Screwtape Letters*, ch 15, para 3.
8. ibid., ch 12, para 5.
9. *Book of Common Prayer*, 'Collect for the 4th Sunday after Trinity'.
10. *The Last Battle,* ch 13, para 32.
11. ibid., ch 15, para 36.
12. ibid.
13. Isaiah 9:2.
14. Luke 4:18.
15. John 10:20.
16. Luke 9:24; also Matthew 10:39, 16:25; Mark 8:35; Luke 17:33; John 12:25.
17. *The Screwtape Letters*, ch 13, para 5.
18. *The Last Battle*, ch 15, para 37.
19. ibid., ch 13, para 32.

Week Two: Living with the beyond

1. *Surprised by Joy*, ch 1, paras 14–16.
2. Wordsworth, 'Lines composed above Tintern Abbey'.
3. Kenneth Grahame, *The Wind in the Willows*, ch 7, para 28.
4. *American Beauty*, screenplay, p. 88.
5. *The Problem of Pain*, ch 1, para 10.
6. *Surprised by Joy,* ch 5, para 10.
7. *Mere Christianity*, book 4, ch 3, para 8.
8. *The Great Divorce*, p. 115.
9. *Mere Christianity*, book 3, ch 10, para 5.
10. ibid, book 3, ch 11, para 6.
11. *The Problem of Pain*, ch 7, para 7.
12. Matthew 6:19–20, 33.
13. Augustine of Hippo, *Lion Dictionary of Christian Quotations*.
14. *The Last Battle*, ch 15, para 39.
15. *The Great Divorce*, p. 25.
16. *Paradise Lost*, 1667, book 1, 1.302.
17. *The Great Divorce*, pp. 62–3.

18. ibid., p. 9.
19. ibid., pp. 7–8.
20. *Mere Christianity*, Preface, para 4.
21. Matthew 25:41.
22. *The Great Divorce*, p. 110.
23. ibid.

Week Three: Living with the unexplained

1. *The Problem of Pain*, ch 6, para 16.
2. ibid.
3. ibid., ch 3, para 8.
4. *A Grief Observed*, ch 3, para 17.
5. *Letters of C. S. Lewis*, 31 January, pp. 237–8.
6. *The Problem of Pain*, ch 6, para 16.
7. *The Problem of Pain,* ch 2, para 13.
8. ibid., ch 2, paras 15–16.
9. *The Problem of Pain,* ch 1, para 3.
10. ibid., p. 81.
11. John 10:10–11, 18.
12. *The Problem of Pain*, ch 3, para 14.
13. *Mere Christianity*, book 2, ch 5, para 2.
14. ibid., book 2, ch 2, para 5.
15. ibid., book 2, ch 2, para 2.
16. ibid., book 2, ch 4, para 4.
17. ibid., book 2, ch 4, para 3.
18. *The Lion, the Witch and the Wardrobe*, ch 15, para 37.

Week Four: Living with what we've been given

1. *Mere Christianity*, book 3, ch 3, para 4.
2. ibid., book 3, ch 3, para 4.
3. ibid., book 3, ch 3, para 8.
4. ibid., book 4, ch 8, paras 2–4.
5. Matthew 5:48.
6. *Mere Christianity*, book 4, ch 8, para 9.
7. Job 2:10.
8. Luke 11:9–13.
9. *Perelandra (Voyage to Venus)*, ch 5, para 103.
10. Romans 7:19.
11. Romans 7:24.
12. Acts 15:38.

13. 2 Corinthians 12:7.
14. 2 Corinthians 12:20.
15. *A Grief Observed*, ch 1, para 24.
16. ibid., ch 1, para 25.
17. *The Screwtape Letters*, ch 8, para 4.
18. 1 Thessalonians 5:18.
19. *Reflections on the Psalms*, ch 9, para 5.
20. ibid., ch 9, para 5.

Week Five: Living with absence

1. *A Grief Observed*, ch 1, para 12.
2. ibid., ch 1, para 7.
3. ibid., ch 1, para 9.
4. ibid., ch 2, para 23.
5. ibid., ch 3, para 25.
6. ibid., ch 3, para 2.
7. Matthew 27:46.
8. Matthew 5:4.
9. *The Lion, the Witch and the Wardrobe*, ch 17, para 70.
10. John 10:10.
11. *The Silver Chair*, ch 2, para 53.
12. *The Screwtape Letters*, ch 8, para 5.
13. Matthew 10:1, 5–10, 16.
14. Mark 3:17.
15. *Mere Christianity*, book 3, ch 2, para 4.
16. George McDonald, quoted in *Mere Christianity*, book 4, ch 9, para 5.
17. *Mere Christianity*, book 3, ch 4, para 8.
18. ibid., book 3, ch 5, para 12.
19. *The Screwtape Letters*, ch 8, para 5.
20. *Mere Christianity*, book 4, ch 11, para 10.
21. ibid., book 4, ch 11, para 15.

Holy Week: Meditative Service

1. *Miracles*, ch 4, paras 5–7.
2. ibid.
3. ibid., ch 14, para 2
4. *Christian Reflections*: 'Modern Theology and Biblical Criticism', para 5.
5. *Letters of C. S. Lewis*, 1947, para 3.

6. John 12:23–24, 32.
7. *Mere Christianity*, book 4, ch 5, para 1.
8. ibid., book 4, ch 5, para 8.
9. Luke 9:23–24.
10. *Mere Christianity*, book 4, ch 11, para 15.
11. Adapted from the *Book of Offices of the British Methodist Church*, 1936.
12. *Till We Have Faces*, part 2, ch 2.
13. John 10:10.
14. *Prince Caspian*, ch 10, para 42.
15. *The Last Battle*, ch 16, paras 30, 33–34.21. 'The Weight of Glory'.

Optional Extra: Living in a Sceptical Age (Prince Caspian)

1. *Good News* version.
2. Jean-Françoise Lyotard, *The Post-Modern Condition*, 1984, pxxiv.
3. *Christian Reflections*: 'Modern Theology and Biblical Criticism', para 25.
4. Don Cupitt, *Creation out of Nothing,* SCM Press, 1990, p. 45.
5. Letters of C. S. Lewis to Arthur Greeves, 24 December 1930, para 9.
6. *Miracles,* p. 137.
7. *Prince Caspian,* ch 11, para 8.
8. 1 Corinthians 3:18 referred to in *Christian Reflections*: 'Christianity and Culture', para 61.
9. Psalm 1:3.
10. Luke 7:35.
11. Robert Frost, 'The Road not Taken', *Mountain Interval*, 1916.
12. 2 Corinthians 5:7.
13. *Christian Reflections*: 'Religion: Reality or Substitute', para 10.
14. *Mere Christianity*, book 3, ch 11, para 5.
15. J. B. Phillips, *Your God is Too Small*, 1961, Introduction, para 1.
16. 2 Peter 3:18.
17. *Chronicles of Narnia: Prince Caspian* screenplay.
18. *Prince Caspian*, ch 10, para 67.
19. *The Screwtape Letters*, ch 8, para 4.
20. *The World's Last Night*: 'On Obstinacy of Belief'.

For Further Reading

This is not an exhaustive list. Besides the volumes listed here, Lewis also wrote a large number of essays and letters on philosophical or Christian topics, some of which have been published as collections, both during his lifetime and afterwards. He also wrote a great deal on his academic speciality of literature, including works on criticism, poetry and medieval and renaissance writings. There are also several more biographies or reference works on Lewis, of necessity I selected just a few.

WORKS BY C. S. LEWIS

Children's fiction: *The Chronicles of Narnia*

The Lion, the Witch and the Wardrobe (1950)
First to be published, though second in the plot. Four children step through a wardrobe into a wintry land in the grip of an evil witch. Their task is to free the land on behalf of Aslan.

Prince Caspian (1951)
The second book published, though fourth in chronological order. Peter, Susan, Edmund and Lucy are called back to Narnia to help Prince Caspian win back the kingdom.

The Voyage of the Dawn Treader (1952)
Edmund, Lucy and their cousin Eustace take to sea with King Caspian and the mouse Reepicheep on a journey to the end of the world.

The Silver Chair (1953)
Eustace Scrubb and Jill Pole find a door to Narnia, where Aslan

gives them the task of helping the lost prince Rilian escape from
Underland, with the help of Puddleglum.

The Magician's Nephew (1955)
The beginnings of the history of Narnia, with echoes of biblical cre-
ation. Digory and Polly discover parallel worlds, meet the evil queen
Jadis and watch as Narnia is breathed into life.

The Horse and His Boy (1956)
The fifth published, but third in Narnian history, this story is about
a talking horse and a boy and their adventures as they run away from
the southern country of Calormen.

The Last Battle (1956)
The final book, this tells of the last great Narnia battle between good
and evil. Eustace and Jill are called back to help King Tirian save the
Narnians from a false Aslan.

Adult fiction

The Pilgrim's Regress (1933)
Reworking of Bunyan's *Pilgrim's Progress*. The hero is hindered on
his journey by various modern philosophies, and finds Joy and Truth
where he least expects.

Out of the Silent Planet (1938)
First of Lewis's space-trilogy, a 'philosophical adventure'. The hero
is kidnapped and taken to Mars as a human sacrifice. He escapes but
returns to face his captors.

Perelandra (also known as *Voyage to Venus*) (1943)
The second of Lewis's space-trilogy. Ransom is taken to an innocent
Eden-like planet where an Eve character is being tempted by an evil
intruder, a scientist from Earth.

That Hideous Strength (1945)
The third of Lewis's space-trilogy. Back in England, a power-mad
bureaucracy aims to control all aspects of nature but succeeds only
in creating a modern Tower of Babel.

The Screwtape Letters (1942)

A compilation of letters from a devil named Screwtape to his nephew Wormwood, an inexperienced tempter, takes a humorous look at sin and the human condition.

The Great Divorce (1945)

Inspired by Dante's *Inferno* – when the citizens of Hell, a self-inflicted nothing, are taken on a bus ride to Heaven, a place of fullness and delight, many of them refuse to stay.

Till We Have Faces (1956)

Retelling the myth of Cupid and Psyche, this story of two princesses, one ugly, one beautiful, tells of the need to find one's self or soul, in order to look the gods in the face.

Non-fiction

The Problem of Pain (1940)

Not an examination of the feelings of pain but an objective answer to the oft-asked question, 'If God is good and omnipotent, why is there pain and evil in the world?'

Mere Christianity (1952)

Compilation and enlargement of talks first broadcast by the BBC during the Second World War, in which Lewis defends Christianity and explains the core of Christian beliefs.

Reflections on the Psalms (1958)

Lewis looks at the worldview of the psalmists on issues such as Nature, Praise and the Law, and tackles head on some difficult questions, such as the validity of cursing enemies.

The Four Loves (1960)

An insightful analysis of four different forms of love as defined in the Greek language: affection, friendship, erotic love and godly love.

Letters to Malcolm: Chiefly on Prayer (1964)

The last of Lewis's works. Written as a series of letters to a close friend, not a 'how to' of prayer, but a wise and honest look at the need for prayer, its problems and joys.

Autobiography

Surprised by Joy (1955)
Lewis describes his search for joy and spiritual truth through his childhood and teens to his conversion from atheism to Christianity in his early thirties.

A Grief Observed (1961)
Published originally under a pseudonym, this is a painfully honest account of Lewis's struggles with grief and loss of faith following the death of his wife Joy.

WORKS ABOUT C. S. LEWIS

Biographies

Lenten Lands by Douglas Gresham
A personal account by Lewis's stepson.

C. S. Lewis: A Biography by Walter Hooper and Roger Lancelyn Green
'Official' version by friends of Lewis, factually accurate but a bit superficial.

Jack: C. S. Lewis and His Times by George Sayer
An excellent part-memoir and part biography by a friend and pupil of Lewis.

Shadowlands by Brian Sibley
Short biography covering Lewis's last years and marriage to Joy.

C. S. Lewis: A Biography by A. N. Wilson
An entertaining but more critical and controversial account of Lewis.

Reference works

C. S. Lewis: A Companion and Guide by Walter Hooper
A hefty definitive reference book including biography and guide to Lewis's writings.

C. S. Lewis Index **edited by Janine Goffar**
A comprehensive dictionary of Lewis quotations.

The Quotable Lewis **edited by Wayne Martindale and Jerry Root**
A selection of quotes on a wide range of topics from Lewis's writings.

The C. S. Lewis Encyclopedia **by Colin Duriez**
A comprehensive guide to Lewis's life, thought and writings.